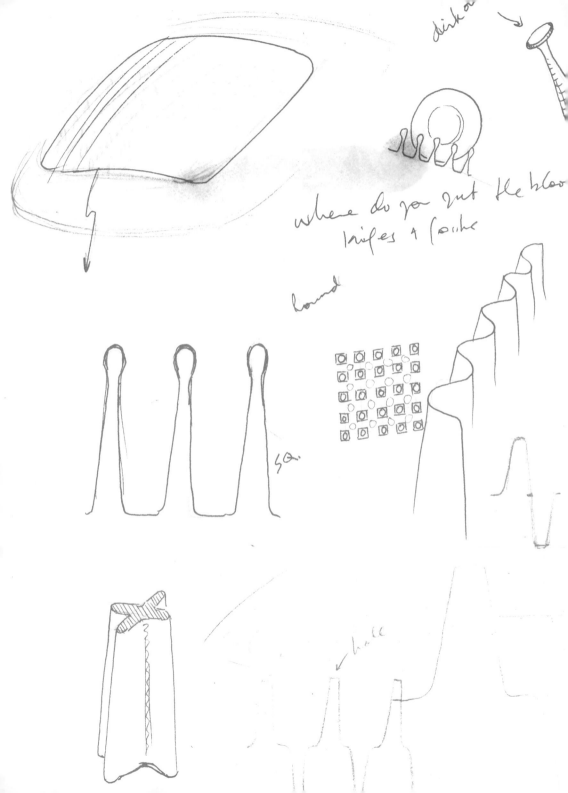

where do you put the knives + forks

round

sq.

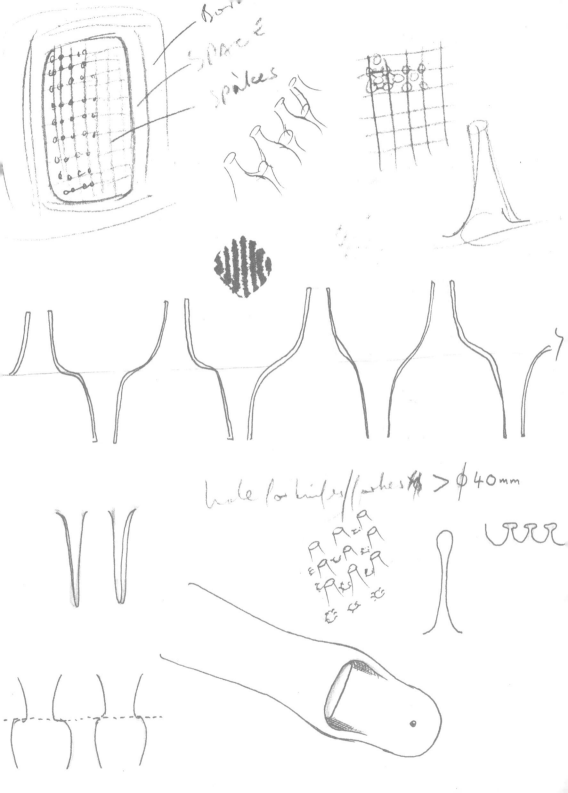

Bon...
Space
spikes

hole for hinge//spokes ∰ > φ40mm

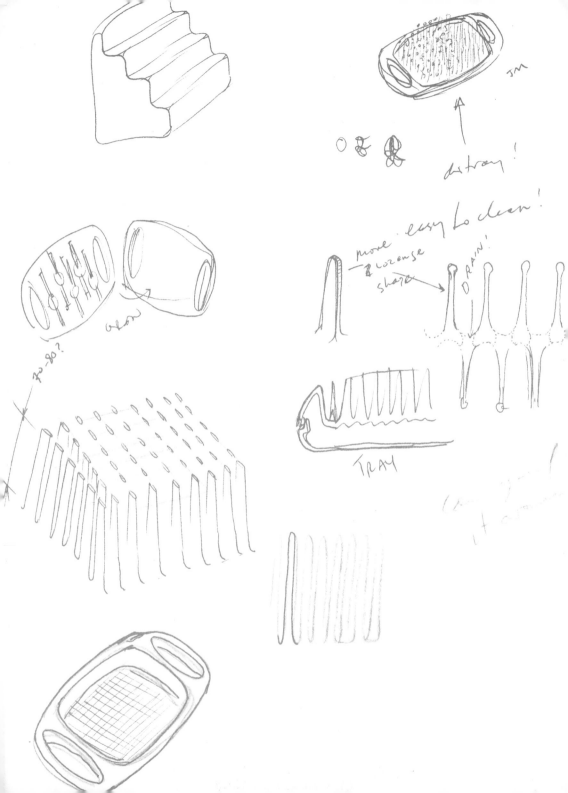

JM

ditray!

more easy to clean!
& lozenge
shape

DRAIN!

TRAY

clean

70-80?

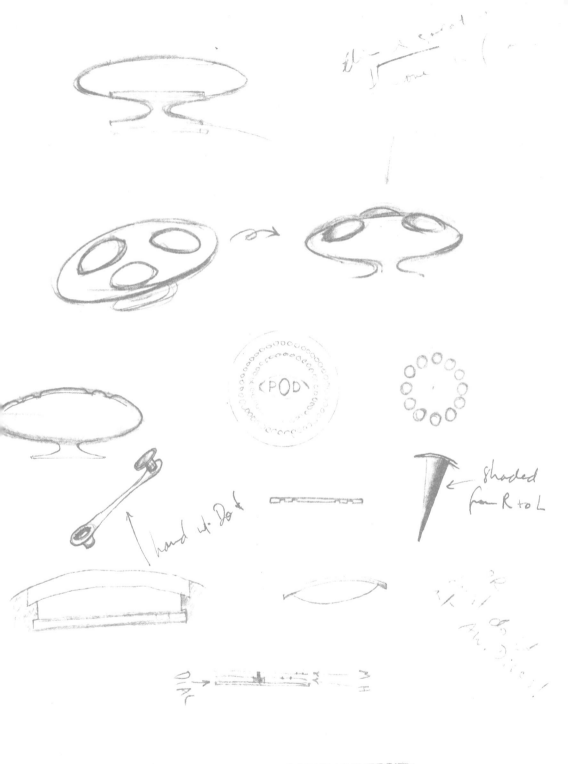

shaded from R to L

hand to Do

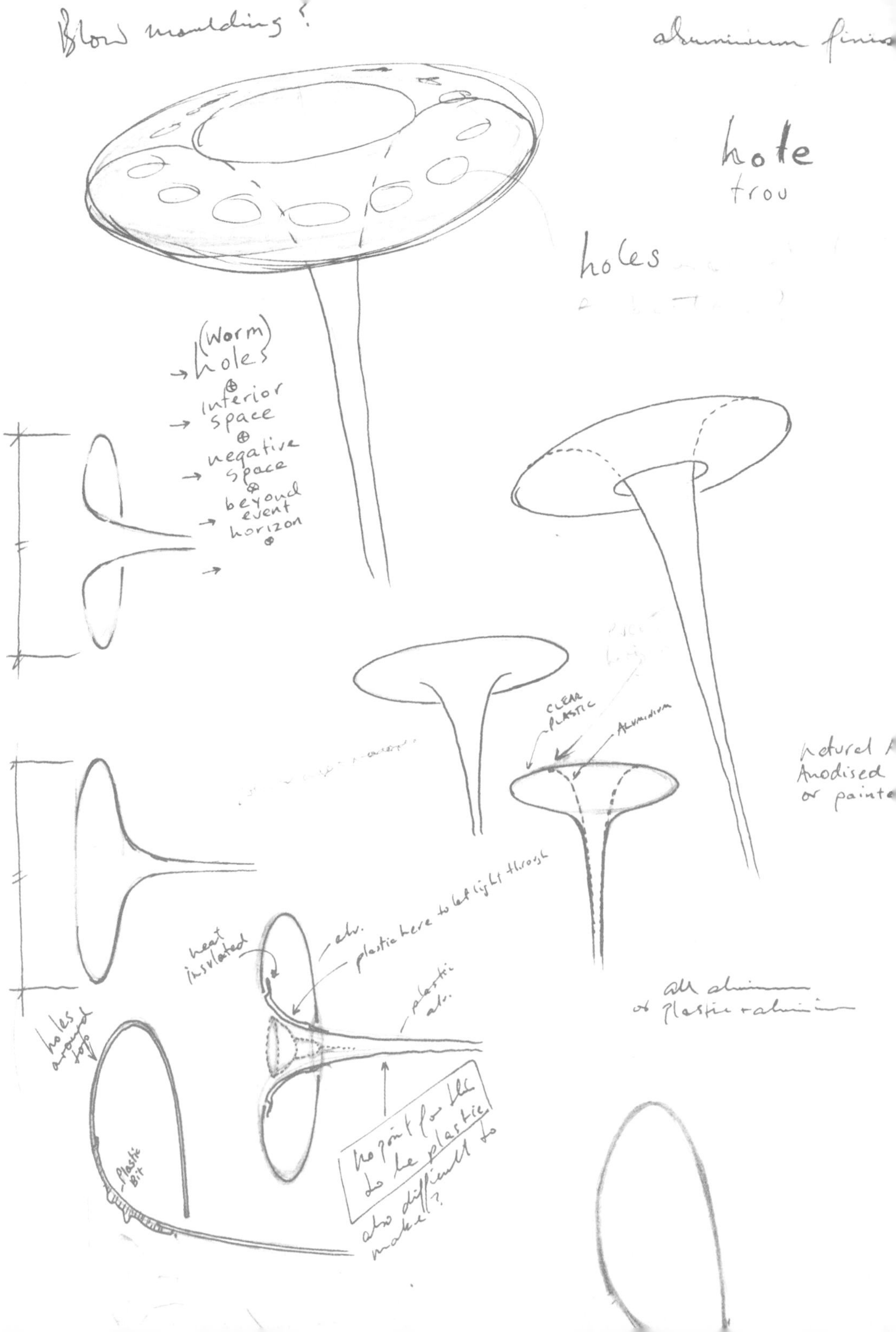

Blow moulding?   aluminium finish

hole
trou

holes

(Worm)
holes
→ holes
        ⊕
→ interior
   space
        ⊕
→ negative
   space
        ⊕
→ beyond
   event
   horizon
        ⊕
→

CLEAR
PLASTIC

ALUMINIUM

natural A
Anodised
or painte

heat
insulated   alu.
                plastic here to let light through

                       plastic
                       alu.

holes
around top

plastic
bit

all aluminium
or plastic + aluminium

the point for the
to be plastic
also difficult to
make?

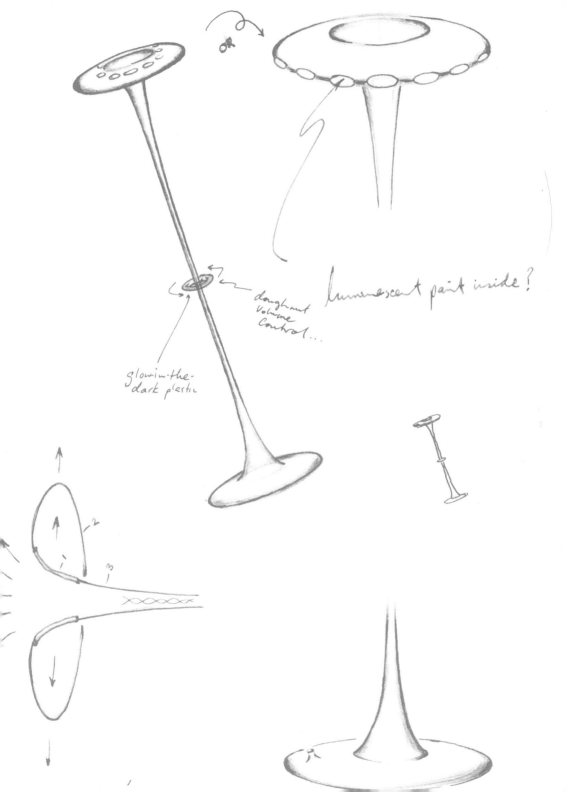

luminescent paint inside?

doughnut
volume
control...

glow-in-the-
dark plastic

HELLO

knurled

Automatic
movement

WINDER

WINDOW TO
MOVEMENT

like this is nice

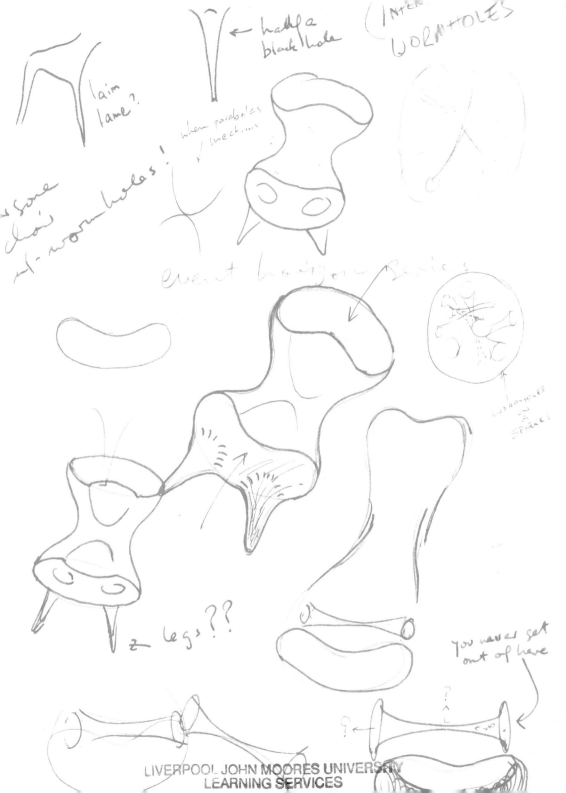

half a black hole

INTER WORMHOLES

I aim lame?

Some droit of worm-holes!

when parabolas intersect...

event horizon Series

WORMHOLES IN A SPHERE!

2 legs??

you never get out of here

?

?

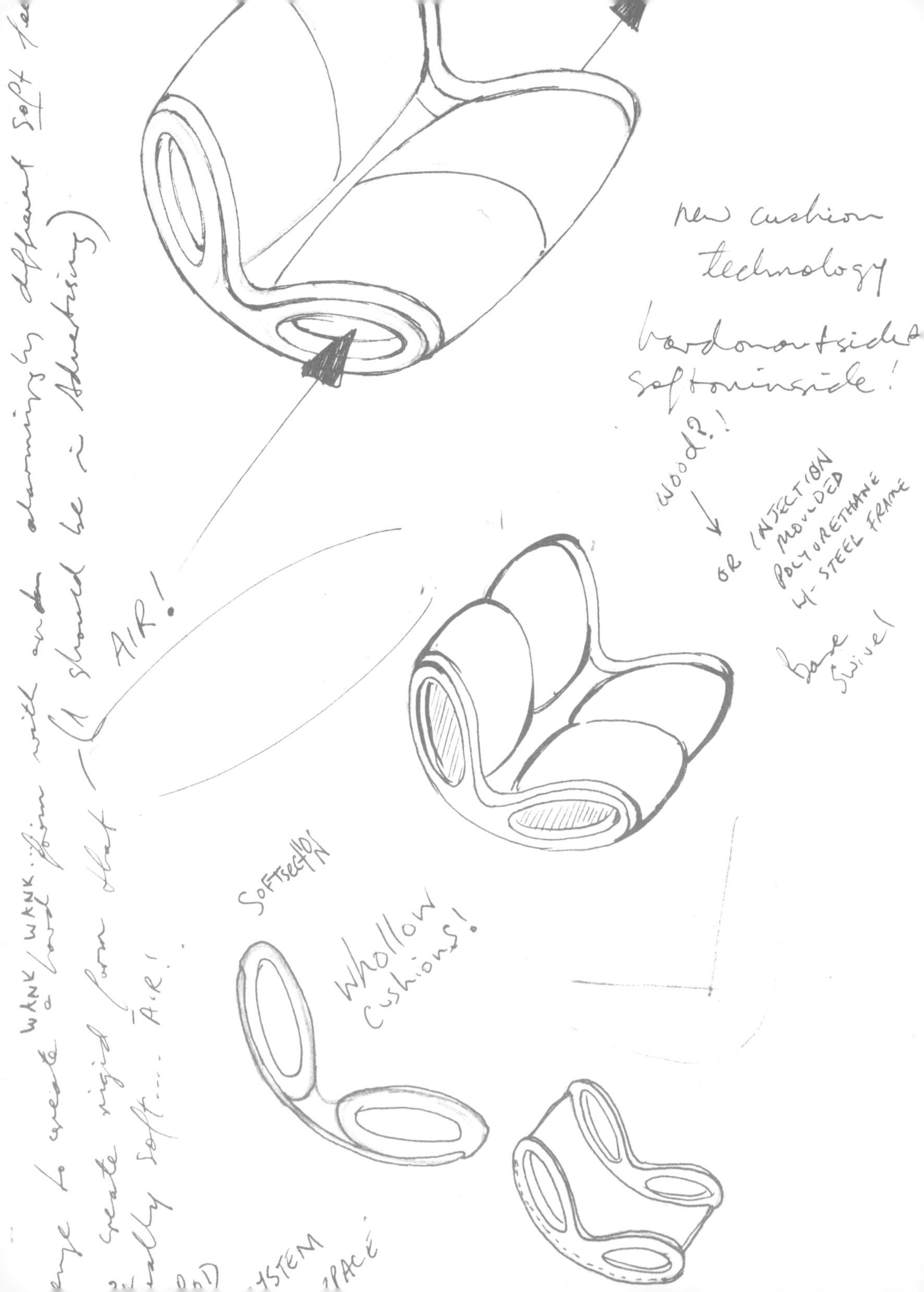

new cushion
technology

hard on outside
soft on inside!

wood?.!

OR INJECTION
MOULDED
POLYURETHANE
W- STEEL FRAME

Base
Swivel

AIR!

SOFTSECTION

Whollow
cushions!

AIR!

... WINK/WINK form with under
(I should be in Advertising)
...eye to create a...form with under... alumium by different soft ...
...create rigid form that
...ally soft.... A.R.!

ROD   SYSTEM   SPACE

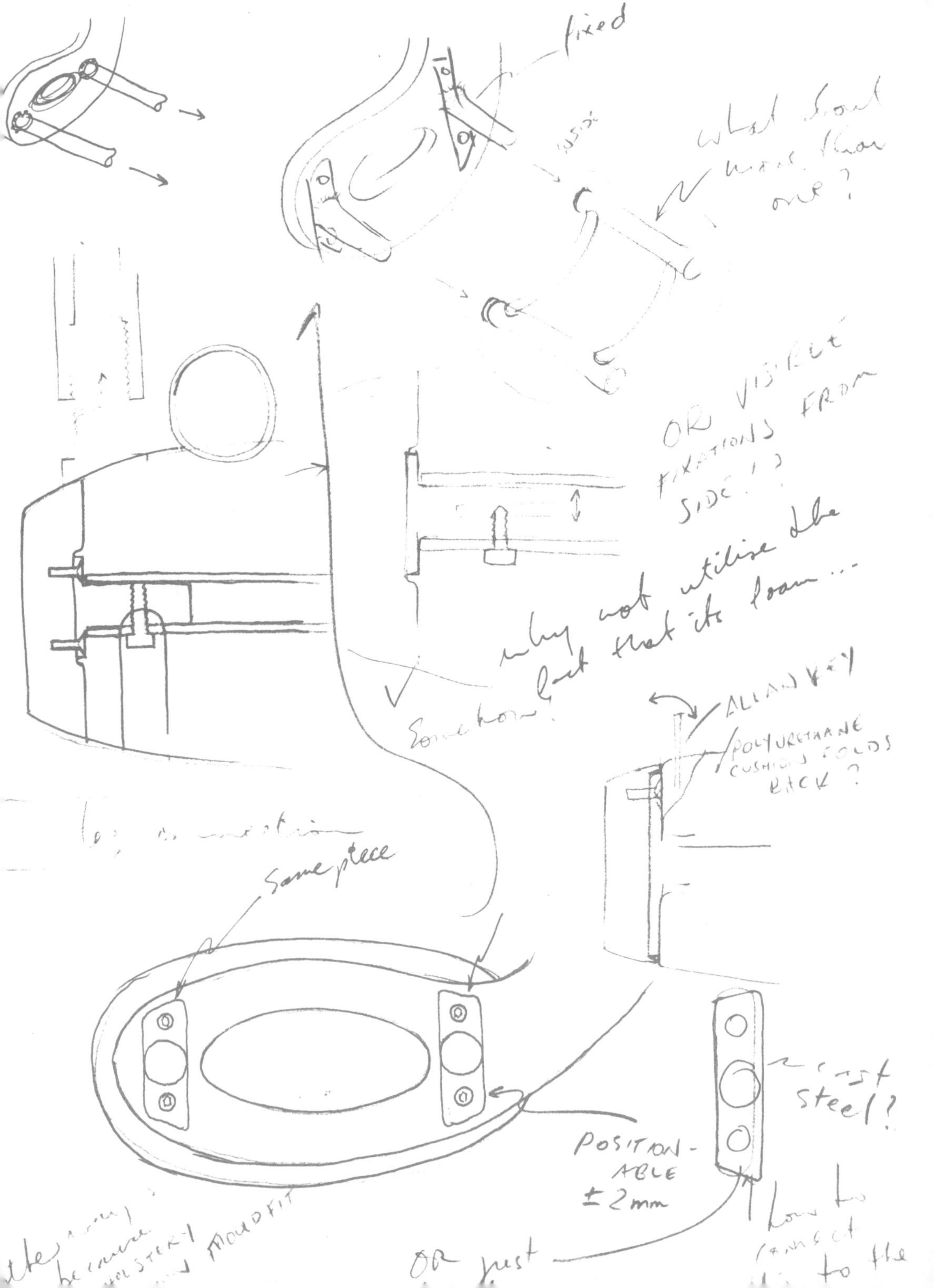

fixed

what Soul
wore thou
one?

OR VISIBLE
FIXATIONS FROM
SIDE ?

why not utilise the
Somehow fact that its foam...

ALLAN KEY
POLYURETHANE
CUSHION FOLDS
BACK ?

Same piece

POSITION-
ABLE
±2mm

cast
steel?

OR just

MOULDFIT

machined out of solid
should be made like this:

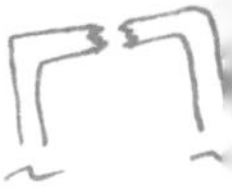

→ then Bolt will fit in line (true)

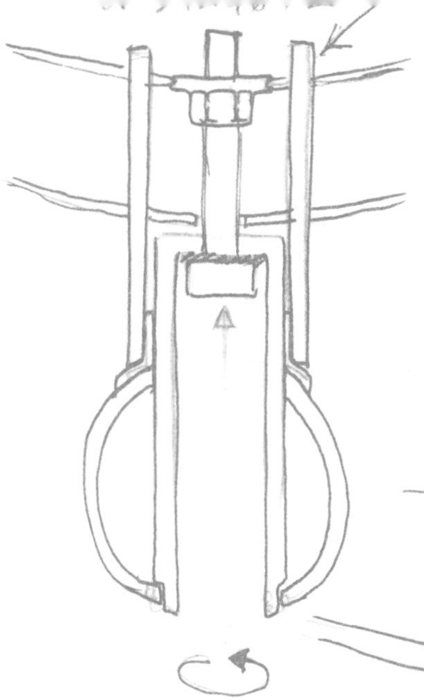

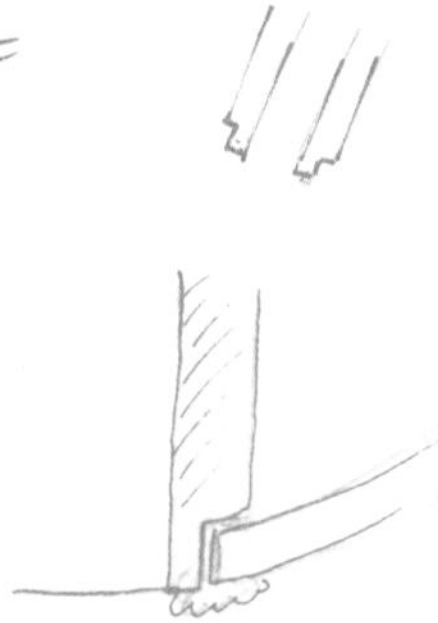

last day OCTOBER
1st week NOV...

DOUG BIRO L.A.
Four Seasons Hotel

310 859 3874

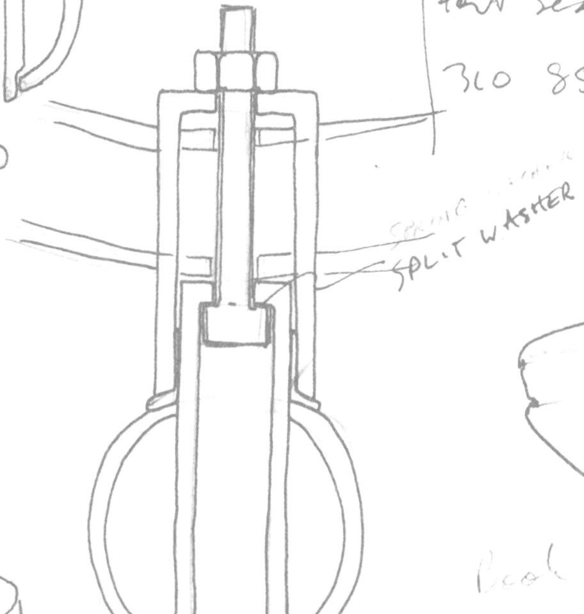
SPRING WASHER
SPLIT WASHER

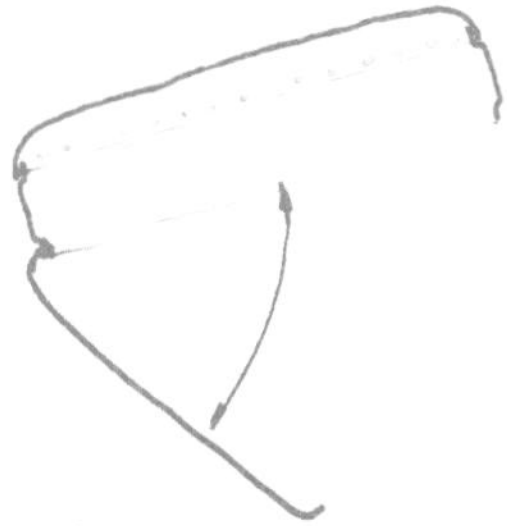

Book notes

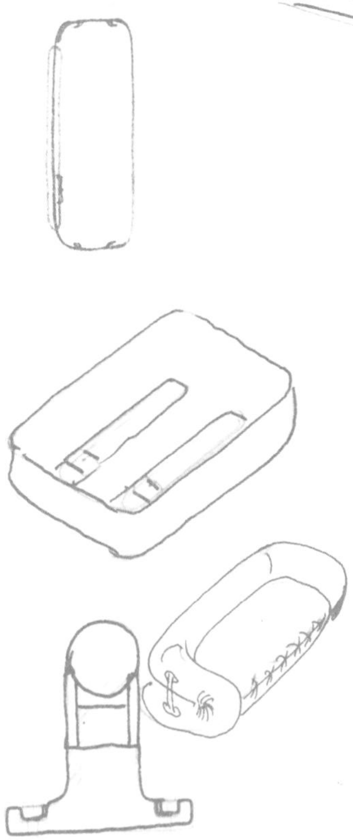

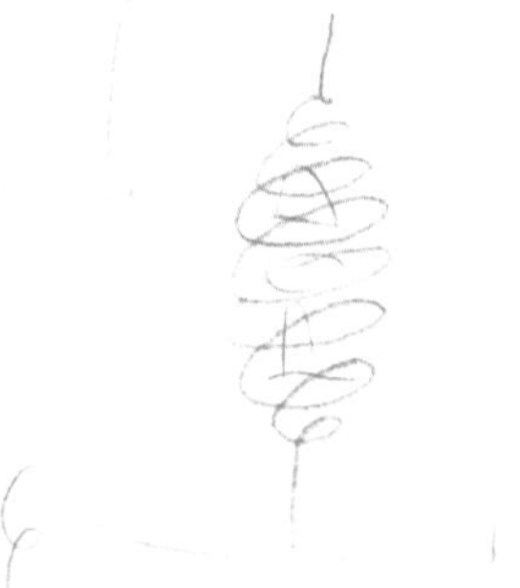

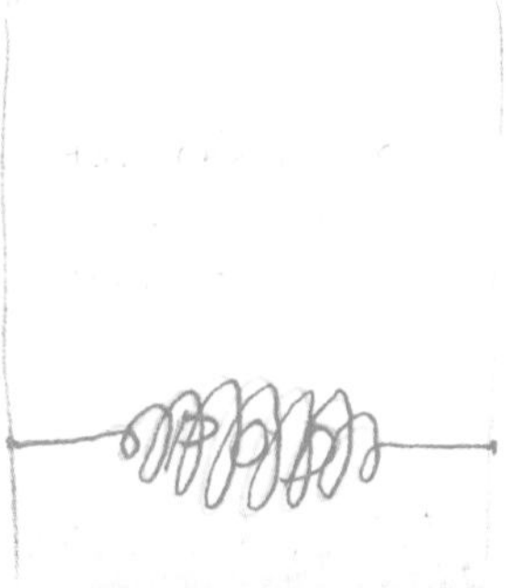

60 155

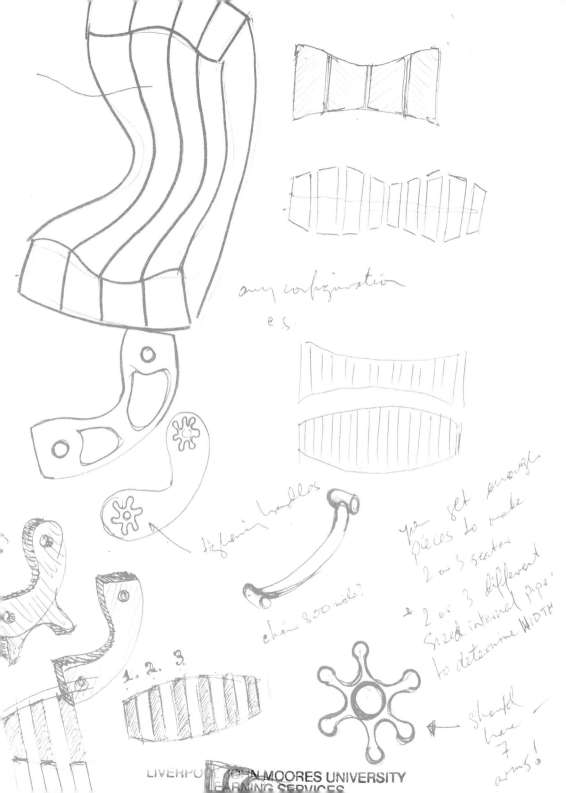

any configuration
e.s.

tightening handles

chain 800 wide?

you get enough
pieces to make
2 or 3 seater

* 2 or 3 different
sized internal pipes
to determine WIDTH

← should
have
7
arms!

1. 2. 3.

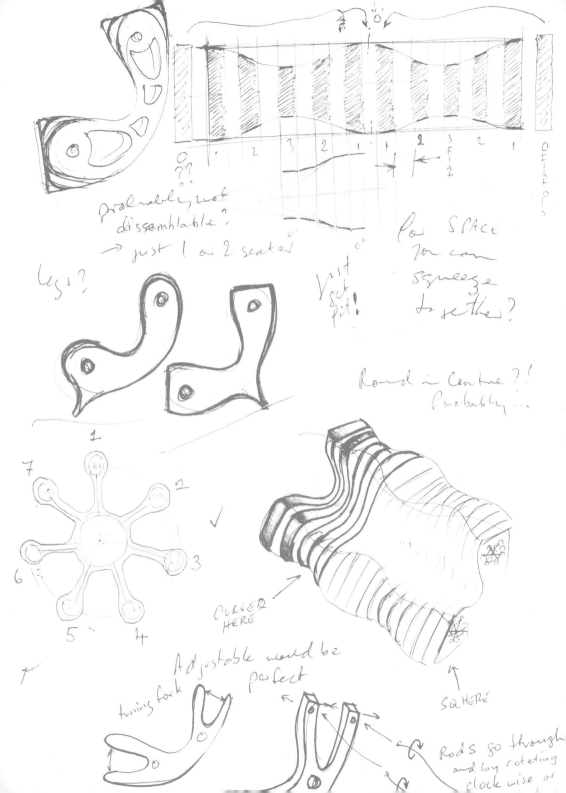

Probably not
dissemblable?
→ just 1 or 2 seater

Legs?

?? ?

Flat

0
1 2 3 2 1 1 2 3 2 1 O flaps?

Just
set
fit!

For SPACE
you can
squeeze
together?

Round in Centre ?!
Probably...

1
7   2

3

6

5   4

✓

CURVED
HERE

SQ. HERE

Adjustable would be perfect
tuning fork

Rod's go through
and by rotating
clockwise or

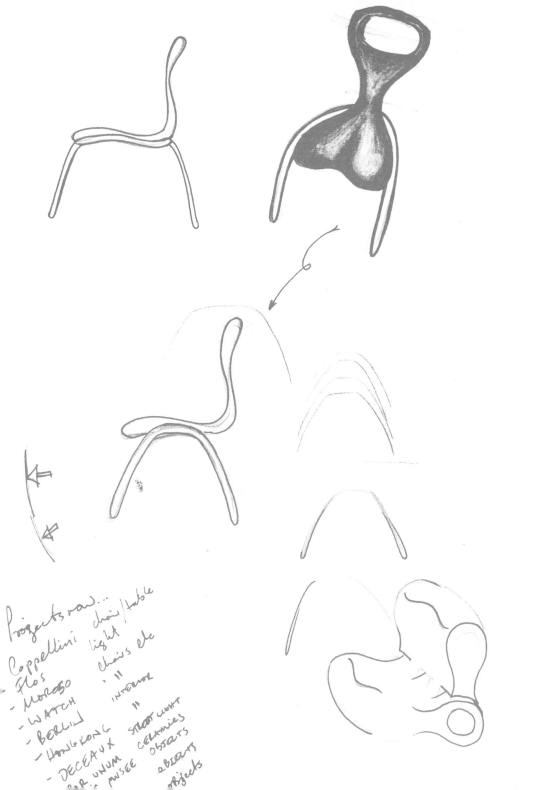

Projects now...
Coppellini chair/table
- FLOS   light
- MOROSO   chairs etc
- WATCH   "   "
- BERLIN   interior
- HONGKONG   "
- DECEAUX   Street light
- PER UNUM ceramics
        MUSEE objets
              objects

tubby

transluscent
polycarbonate

Marc Newson.

Conway Lloyd Morgan

⟲ Thames & Hudson

Marc Newson
Conway Lloyd Morgan

First published in the
United Kingdom in 2003 by
Thames & Hudson Ltd,
181A High Holborn,
London WC1V 7QX

British Library Cataloguing
-in-Publication Data
A catalogue record for this book is
available from the British Library

ISBN 0-500-28318-4

Printed in Italy

Contents

Marc Newson
Conway Lloyd Morgan

Starting Here

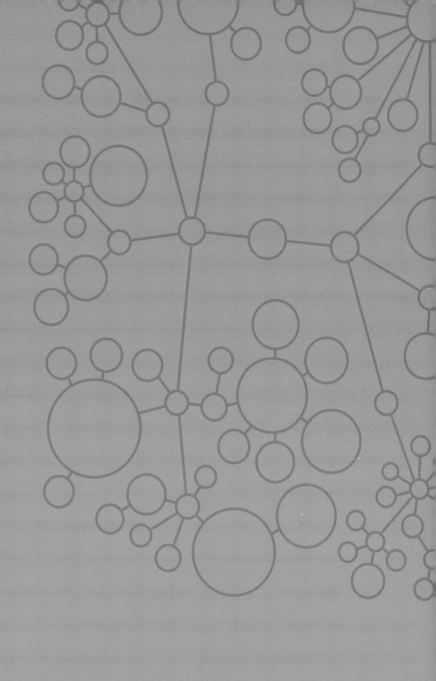

—   Where might one have chosen
to be born, in the early 1960s, to have some chance of growing
up amid contemporary furniture, design, and art? Central London,
perhaps, Manhattan, or Los Angeles, Rome, or Milan, Paris even.
Probably not Sydney, the chief port of Australia. Rome was still
the city of the elegant decadence of La Dolce Vita, Milan defined
the new domestic landscape, Paris was the home of Corbusier,
Picasso and Sartre, America the place, as the song said, where
everyone wanted to be. London was Biba, boutiques and
Beatlemania. But Australia?

—   One epitome of the image
of Australia was Bazza McKenzie, the cartoon-strip figure in the
London satirical magazine 'Private Eye'. Bazza, with his absurd
and incomprehensible vocabulary, bush hat and cans of Foster's
lager, who shambled about the streets of London, failing to get
laid or otherwise engage in meaningful contact with the world
around him. A brilliant parody of what would later be called the
backpacker, Bazza's antics made his audience feel they had the
measure of the Antipodeans. In fact the rich inventiveness of his
language alone shows that the parody is by no means one-sided:
the swinging Londoners he encounters are showed up as equally
foolish. And Bazza's creator, Barry Humphries, was considerably
more sophisticated than his invention. His subsequent career
as a wickedly satirical comedian in drag understates his profound
knowledge of European art and culture.

—   Other signs showed that
Australia was not just beer and baa-lambs (the wool trade had
made Australia a wealthy country in the 1950s and 1960s).
The Sydney Opera House, on which construction started in the
sixties, became an overnight architectural icon, and marked an
end to the "cultural cringe." In the mid-1960s Jack Brabham
dominated the European Grand Prix motor racing circuit in a car
designed in Australia by Ron Tauranac, with an Australian engine
by Repco. And the end of the conservative Menzies era in the
late 1960s paved the way for a cultural renaissance, particularly in
cinema. Directors like Peter Weir ('Picnic at Hanging Rock'),
Gillian Armstrong ('My Brilliant Career'), George Miller ('Mad Max')
and Ken Hannam ('Sunday Too Far Away') reached an
international audience and offered it a new vision of Australia. One
of the first films of this era was, appropriately enough, Bruce
Beresford's 'The Adventures of Barry McKenzie'.

—   Marc Newson was born in
Hornsby, near Sydney, in 1963. His father disappeared soon after
he was born, so he and his mother lived with her parents. Not an
auspicious start. But his mother got a job with a firm of modernist
architects, Petitt & Sevitt, and then, through them, became the
manager of a modern hotel on the Pacific coast. As Newson
explained to Alice Rawsthorn in her book 'Marc Newson', "through
her working for these architects, we had some exposure to

24   Marc Newson,
        2001, portrait
        by John Ross

Marc Newson
—   Starting Here

modern architecture, because she got to know about Corbu and stuff. And she had really good taste, so whenever she bought anything for the house it would be one of those plastic Danese calendars or something by Enzo Mari. And the hotel was an amazing place on the most beautiful beach, insanely deluxe and stuffed with really cool furniture brought over from Italy – Joe Colombo trolleys, Sacco bean bags and cane seats hanging from the ceiling. I was too young to register why it was so cool, but it all made a huge impression on me." Marc and his mother traveled in Europe for a year when he was a young teenager, and upon their return she remarried and they went with her new husband, George Conomos, to South Korea for three years, before Newson returned to Australia to attend boarding school. He then went to the Sydney College of Arts to study jewelry. Not, as he has explained, because he wanted to become a jeweler or silversmith, but because he wanted to learn how to make things. In the end he spent his time making furniture, convincing his teachers that furniture is made for bodies to use in just the same way jewelry is.

—   Despite this unusual upbringing, Newson resolutely identifies himself as Australian. Or more precisely, as having an Australian attitude. As he says, "Australia's a big country with only a few people living in it, so it hasn't got a lot of formal culture, despite some fine architects such as Glenn Murcutt. And most white Australians don't have much time for the indigenous culture of Australia, though I have always been fascinated by it. So I didn't have a whole lot of design history rammed down my throat – I was at an art school anyway. But what Australia does have is a history of invention, often driven by necessity. There's a parallel with the Soviet Union here: Australia's the same only less sophisticated, and with more sunshine! But take someone like Jack Brabham building his winning racing car in his backyard." Australian popular culture, which on the contrary, Newson asserts, is strong, also shares that bent for technology and invention. "Take surfboards: there's no book on the subject, but a lot of kids know how to build one of the things. And there are details to the form and the shape which make a difference to performance. Whether the board has two or three fins, for example, and other subtleties which are almost imperceptible, play an immense part in how the board behaves in the water. So you could say I studied silversmithing and jewelry not because I wanted to work with precious metals but because I wanted to know how to use the machinery, how to weld, how to use a lathe, how to build things. I had to train myself to make things because there weren't that many places to go and get things made the way I wanted."

—   While a student, Newson worked to earn money in a news service agency in the King's Cross area of Sydney, where he saw all the European lifestyle and design magazines such as 'Domus' and 'Ottagono', 'Casa Vogue' and 'Flash Art', which brought him up to date on design in Europe, and in the college library he read books on the Bauhaus and the California design tradition of Saarinen and Eames. These points o

Marc Newson
—   Starting Here

—   Sydney Opera House
—   Biomega
—   Ikepod
—   Vidal Sassoon

28   Orgone Lounge
       and Citroën DS.

contact gave him a visual awareness of contemporary design, without the intellectual baggage straps of design history, or the design hierarchies and product typologies, which beset European and American design. "The positive aspect of being in Australia, which apart from popular culture–and native culture–was a bit of a vacuum, was that you were free to do your own thing, to choose your own influences. It was an odd place to get trained in, though," he says. "You kind of have to make do in a lot of ways, and because of that I became really interested in technology and in building things. I guess if I hadn't dropped out of a lot of school I'd have ended up learning to be an engineer, probably in aeronautics. That's an area I was passionate about as a kid and I still am interested in now."

—   Putting his technological expertise to work has let him over the last twenty years create cars and bars, furniture and housewares, planes and restaurants, bicycles and bottle stoppers. "People often can't understand how it is that I can work on so many different typologies, how the same person can design a restaurant and design a car and design a bicycle and design a perfume bottle. But for me that's what design is. Design is the ability to tackle all of those things."

quote.

30/1   Olympic Torch
       concept, 1998;
       Stamps produced
       by the Australian
       Postal Service,
       2000

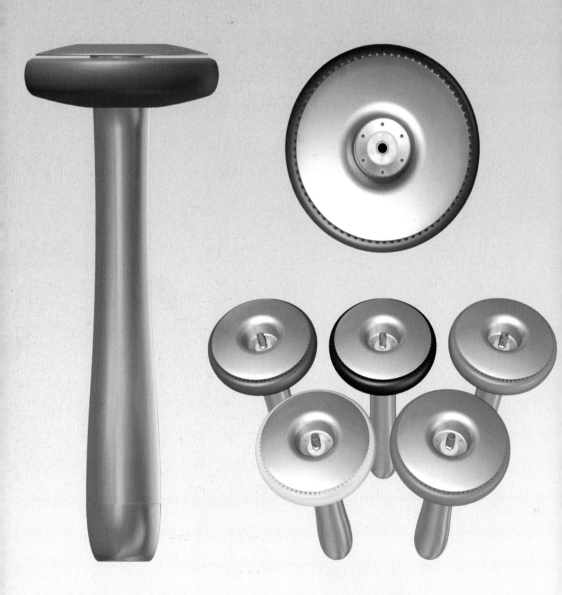

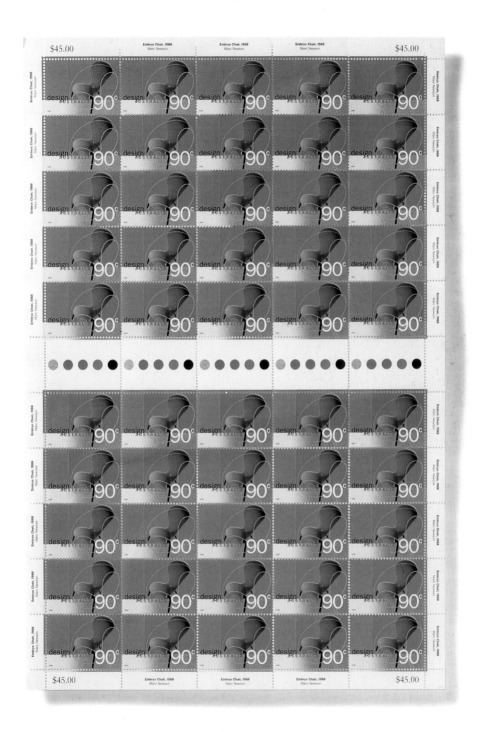

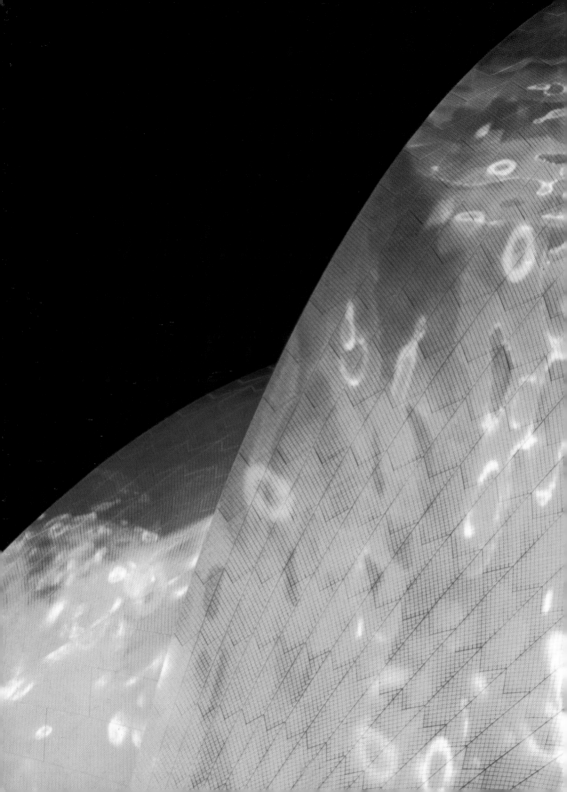

Sydney Opera House

— Back in the old Cold War, black-and-white television days, the author's family was watching the evening news on the BBC. The British Conservative party were holding their annual conference in Brighton, so an image of the Brighton Pavilion appeared on the screen as a header for the event. "Oh no," said my mother, "it's the Kremlin, what's happened now." As the right-wing of the family, my mother was never allowed to forget the remark. But this story may perhaps serve as a warning to those who think of cities in terms of single icons.

— That said, the Sydney Opera House—the drowning nun in local parlance—is about as close to an iconic image as you can get. A literally landmark building, it defined Australia as a new cultural territory, despite a bitter process of design and creation, within which the original architect, Jorn Utson, was ignominiously and unjustifiably fired from the task of completing his design. Nonetheless, it has been an immense success, in terms of positioning Sydney, and so Australia, on the cultural map. So much so that when, some thirty years later, the British architect Terry Farrell was invited to create a design for a new restaurant and bar to sit on reclaimed docklands near the Newcastle New Bridge—itself built as a scale test for the Sydney Harbour Bridge, he unhesitatingly swung some sail shapes onto its roof as a gesture of homage to the Opera House that sits in the shadow of the upscaled version.

— In the year 2000, Sydney also hosted the Olympic Games, and for the concurrent Sydney Festival, a month-long annual arts and music event, it was decided to commission a new lighting scheme for the Opera House. Leo Scofield, director of the Festival, asked Marc Newson to design the scheme. "Scofield is a really interesting guy," Newson comments. "He's very influential in Sydney and in Australia generally; he knows everybody and about everything, and he's great at putting people together and getting things done. If Australia had a Minister of Culture, it'd have to be him! He was almost single-handedly responsible for getting me to do the project, even though I'd no previous experience in the field. As he said, 'this project must have an Australian designer.' And the choice was me."

— The Opera House is a large and complex building, but an existing lighting system with several hundred lamps was in place, with computer controls operated by a mixing desk. What Newson created was a series of four sequences that ran on a continuous loop, each performance lasting about an hour. "It wasn't strictly speaking an animation," Newson explains, "but the images did move, morphing from one into another. The forms were pretty abstract – I really just wanted to drench the whole building in light and color. Each sequence had a theme: fire, water, sky, dreamtime. Fire moved into water through images of a coral reef, for example, and sky and stars into dreamtime."

—   Newson makes the idea seem quite straightforward, but to create the design Newson's team, together with the people at Toast in Sydney, had to input a virtual model of the Opera House on computer and then accurately gauge the color effects of each element in the design. They worked closely with the company that designed the original lighting and mixing system, but modelling a building as complex as the Opera House is still no easy task. It is proof of the success of the system that Newson and de Haan put in place to organize the office's work that the project was completed in a relatively short timescale, and very successfully as well.

—   The Sydney Opera House project was also, in a sense, a formal recognition by Australia of Newson's world status as a designer (unfortunately, another such potential gesture, the commission to design the torch for the Sydney Olympic Games in 2000 did not go to Newson but to another Australian designer; "I guess because I'd left home," Newson comments wryly). Newson's design achievement was also celebrated by a retrospective exhibition from August 2001 to February 2002 in the Powerhouse Museum in Sydney, which has the largest collection of Newson's work, especially his early pieces.

—   Newson's own homage to Australia can be seen, in part, in the work he purchased for the Conran Collection at the Design Museum in London. Each year the Collection invites a well-known designer to select design works up to a value of US$45,000, which is then donated to the Museum. Newson's selection included a surfer's wet suit, two modern surfboards (and a traditional one from California) and a pair of Ugg boots, made of sheepskin and much favored by surfers, and Australia's new plastic banknotes (more for the technology than the design). His acquisitions also included a traditional Japanese knife, sea animal figurines from the Monterey Bay Aquarium and a Russian spacesuit (see page 216).

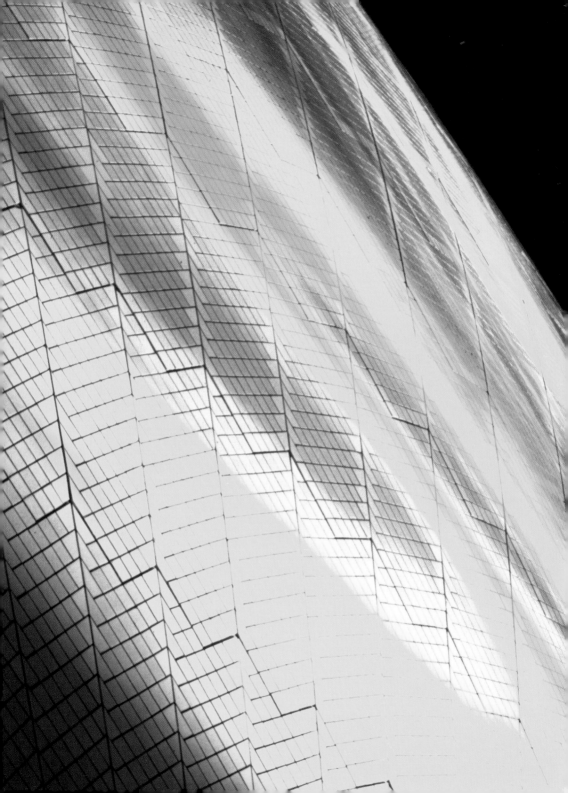

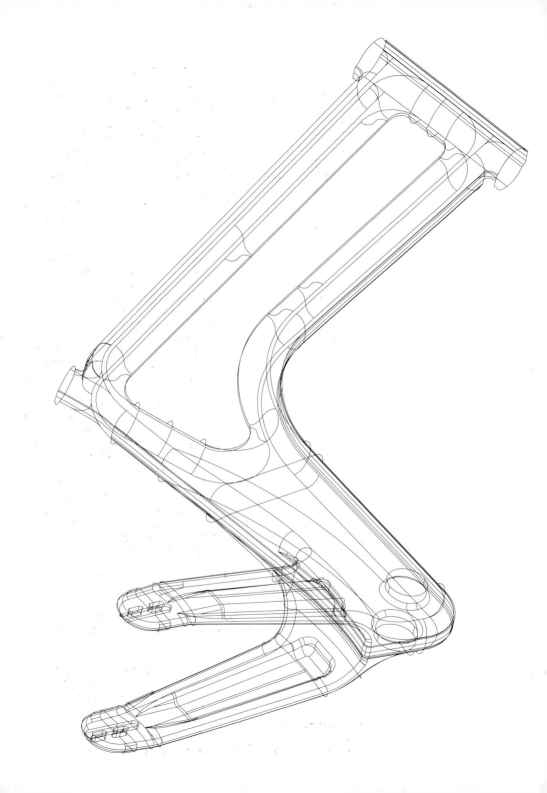

Biomega

42 Detail from
wireframe model
of MN01 cycle,
1988/9

— Copenhagen, in Denmark, is one of the cycling capitals of the world, so not surprisingly it is the home of Biomega, a company started in 1998 to make bicycles. Their original offering was a conventional cycle called the Copenhagen, appropriately enough. And their first original model was designed by Marc Newson. Biomega was founded by two friends from university, Jens Martin Skibsted and Elias Grove Nielsen. Skibsted had been sketching ideas for bicycles ever since a trip to Barcelona in 1991 where he saw Gaudí's fantastic architecture. He had since worked in an art gallery and for a record label in Copenhagen. Nielsen had a sandwich and catering business. The sale of the latter and some family money provided the seed capital for the new company.

— What the two entrepreneurs had realized was that cycling was no longer just a means of transportation. The success of mountain bikes in bringing new users into cycling for fun and exercise had also turned the bicycle into a lifestyle object. Choosing a bike was making a cultural statement, like selecting clothes from a chosen fashion house or furniture by a particular designer. The fact that neither Skibsted nor Nielsen had any experience in the cycle industry was not the point: they understood lifestyle businesses such as music and food. In fact most of their cycle production was and is outsourced.

— Skibsted did not want to use established cycle designers, for the reason that they would be too conventional. He wanted product designers, and Newson was an obvious choice, if only because he had not designed a bike before. What he invited Newson to do was to "explore the limits of bike design." Newson had recently been working with the aviation industry, and had learned about superformed aluminum, which he felt was the right material and process to use, because a much greater fluidity of shape could be achieved. He suggested that the metal elements were bonded together rather than welded, again to maintain the purity of the form. He pressed Skibsted to use this technology for the bike design. For Newson, this kind of technology transfer is a key part of the way he works: "I'm not interested in acquiring all of the stuff that I do, in fact I only own one or two of my own pieces. But what I get at the end of the whole process is the knowledge, of understanding materials and processes." In fact, the experience of Newson and his team in sourcing and managing industrial processes was to be an important contribution to the project.

quote.

44/5 MN01

— Biomega hesitated over the material as well as the bonding process, but as Newson pointed out to them, "if we don't try other ways, then we'll only move forward in the same direction." They consulted the Danish Technological Institute and materials experts at Saab, who recommended Permabond ESP 110 for the bonding, an epoxy resin that was used to attach the jet engines to the Thrust rocket

quote –

car that broke the land speed record in 1997. Even in light of this fact, the company assembling the bikes refused to offer a firm guarantee that the frames would withstand the loads involved.

— The choice of these high-technology materials and processes was not an end in itself, however much they would add to the allure of the finished product. Rather, the technical solution cleared the ground for a new design approach. "I saw designing the bike as an exercise in joining the dots," Newson has said, "and so I looked for the simplest form that was able to do this, to connect the headset to either the bottom bracket or seat and then to the rear wheel. Also, it was of huge importance to me to lose all the superfluous shit and hide all the ugly bits, like the cables." Newson had lots of bikes as a child and even built his own: "I was obsessed with bikes and even raced them," he says, "and so I wanted to create an urban bike for Biomega." There are a limited number of options for a bicycle frame, since they all have to relate to the relative positions of the rider's body. Newson's favored solution is the MN01, an expanded Z shape, neatly profiled, which links front forks and handlebar to the seat with the lower bar of the Z securing the rear wheels. It is elegant and efficient, and all the cables for gears and brakes are hidden inside it.

— Biomega is commissioning more designs from Newson to follow the MN01 and the MN02 with its luminous frame, and is also working with the organic designer Ross Lovegrove on a "fold-flat" cycle that can be hung on a wall—either for storage or display. They are also said to be talking to the designer Jasper Morrison. But these "designer cycles" are not simply exercises in branding, nor only about bringing new technologies to the cycle business. Jonathan Ive, the vice president of industrial design at Apple, who created the iMac, has commented that "the MN01 implies a change of the rules," and as Rico Zorkendorfer, a senior designer in the San Francisco office of the product design firm Ideo points out, "These guys are trying to push the image of bikes and create a lifestyle product. They've reversed the creation process; now design is driving the geometry of the frame, pushing it into new production methods." Newson's bikes should be compared, not so much to other bikes but to products such as the Apple iMac. The iMac justly deserves its many design awards, since it provided a new interpretation of the personal computer, even if the functionality remained largely the same. It goes beyond a design solution into a cultural statement. It offers the user a new way of considering a familiar piece of equipment. In the same way, the success of Newson's design (which won the Summer Hardware category of the 2000 ISPO DuPont BrandNew contest, in which Biomega itself won the main prize as the hottest start-up company) redefines urban cycling.

Ikepod

50 Ikepod Hemipode packaging, 1996

51 Mystery Clock, 1989

51 Large Pod Watch, 1986/7

— Marc Newson tells the story of how, at the age of thirteen or so, he dismantled a wristwatch belonging to his uncle and rebuilt it in a new plastic case. He was always fascinated by the contradiction of small size and technical complexity in watches: one of his first products after finishing college was the Small and Large Pod watches, which he assembled by hand ("a nightmare"). The Large Pod watch uses rotating buttons rather than conventional hands, a concept explored on a wider scale with his Mystery clock, designed in 1989, which uses magnets to hold the buttons in place, a feat requiring careful balance of the magnetic forces.

— In 1993 Newson had an exhibition of his recent furniture work for Cappellini in Frankfurt, where he met Oliver Ike. Ike was managing a contract furnishing business selling "designer furniture" to hotels and restaurants in Germany and Switzerland and he knew Newson's work: he even had seen one of Newson's early watches. As Ike says, "I spent a lot of time doing crazy things, from dealing in real estate in Berlin to selling patents for inventors, and I'd just finished furnishing a new hotel in Switzerland, and met, through the architect, someone who had a watchmaking business. When I went to see Newson I didn't have any plan in mind, I was just interested to meet the guy." But over an evening's conversation Newson suggested to Ike that he design a watch for Ike to manufacture and market. They also decided to form a company between them to create and market the watches Newson would design, calling it Ikepod.

— Despite Orson Welles's disparaging remarks in 'The Third Man' (which he himself introduced into Graham Greene's script) about three hundred years of peace and prosperity in Switzerland only producing the cuckoo clock, until the 1960s the Swiss watch industry was regarded as the best in the world, with the town of La Chaux-de-Fonds as its headquarters. The invention of electrical and digital watches and their proliferation from Japan and Southeast Asia into the lower end of the market in the 1970s nearly overturned this supremacy. The Swatch concept, with its bright colors and modern designs, often art-directed by Alessandro Mendini, rescued the day, at least in commercial terms. But Swatches were also electrical rather than mechanical, and so the traditional luxury market of crafted mechanical watches was if anything left even more isolated, and the term "designer watch" meant inexpensive plastic. The new firm thus faced a considerable challenge, particularly as the manufacture of movements was concentrated in the hands of a small number of firms (only a few of the traditional watchmakers, such as Jaeger-LeCoultre, still make both their own movements and cases).

52   Seaslug Watch,
     1993

53   Tourbillon Watch,
     2000

— What drew Newson to the project was his love of engineering as much as designing. The partners decided from the first that the watches had to be not merely superbly designed but also technically at the top of the range as well. For example they have recently added a watch with a tourbillon movement to the collection. "We aimed to add a new model every year," Newson explains, "and any serious watch collector knows that a tourbillon movement is the ultimate system–a movement within a movement–for chronological accuracy." Serious collectors are at the heart of Ikepod's intended market: "We do sell at the Museum of Modern Art," Newson says, "but that's because other work of mine is in the collection. Selling Ikepod watches in design shops would be the kiss of death, as we see it."

— Look at the watch enthusiasts' forums on the worldwide web and you get the feeling that the world of watch collecting is having a hard time coming to terms with Ikepod. "Surprisingly, I did see an Ikepod once at Brinkhaus" was one posting (referring to a well-established watch dealer in Vancouver). Another posting describes the watches as "zany," another "felt sorry" for them. But both the last two, when they bought and wore Ikepod watches, found themselves liking them a great deal, despite a lingering suspicion of the "design" element. In fact the watches are comfortable to wear and good to look at precisely because they are designed–design is integral to them, not (as some collectors seem to think) some sort of extra. "Getting the watchband on the Hemipode watch just right, so that the watch sat comfortably on the wrist was something I'm really pleased about," according to Newson, "but except for Porsche's work with IWC, very few of the leading watch companies like Omega, Patek Philippe or Cartier had a view of design in the way we understand design now. We put design at the center, and that puts us in a rather bizarre position in the market."

— Being co-owner of the company rather than a designer working for a client, has also given Newson a different perspective. "I design all the watches," he says, "and art-direct and supervise everything the company produces, for example Richard Allan's work on the advertising, but I'm also involved in everything the company does. A designer doesn't often get that sort of viewpoint on the work he does, by participating in every aspect of the business as I do at Ikepod. A lot of things that I would never ever consider when working for a large client, become considerations with Ikepod, and things end up a lot more rational and focused as a result. It's a lot more like the way I used to work in my early twenties, when I didn't have the funds so had to make compromises which in turn drove the design process forward."

54/5   Variant faces for
      the Hemipode
      series

Marc Newson
— Starting Here

— "When at first I went to the Basel Watch Fair, no one had any idea who I was; the name Marc Newson may mean something in design, but not in the Swiss watch industry. That's rather a humbling experience but it's also quite refreshing and exciting to be anonymous, even though we know now that much of the success of the company is because of the design work. And I enjoy being involved, in meeting our distributors and collectors and building relationships with them. So there are things I do for Ikepod that I wouldn't do for other clients. It's very special."

— Ikepod now sell over five thousand watches a year in forty-two different countries, but it has been a considerable battle. "We didn't break even until after four years," Ike points out, "because we were working so hard to build the company. But we're getting there: a few years ago Philip Stern, the head of Patek Philippe, probably thought Ikepod was a soap powder or a washing-up liquid–if he thought about it at all. Now he knows who we are. At first I thought having Marc Newson would be an immediate asset, but in the watch business nobody knows who he is, because designers are not important, brands are." Building the brand is partly a matter of getting the right distributors, partly of putting the products in the right context. For three years, for example, Ikepod sponsored a classic racing car meeting at Watkins Glen in upstate New York, the first US Grand Prix circuit and a "Porsche Clash" for classic Porsches (limited to 911 entrants, a nice touch).

— But above all building the brand is about the total product offer, not about design. For the serious watch collector, the movement is as important as the case or the maker's name. Ikepod began by buying existing movements (a supply factor that limited their growth). "But in each case," Ike points out, "we would adapt the movement both to make the watch individual and to fit the design concept. So we might change the position of the day/date box, traditionally at three o'clock, or relocate one of the secondary dials. This is something Marc and I would work out together, so as to resolve the elements into a satisfactory whole." For the Tourbillon watch they were able to work much more closely with the creators of the movement, the Progress Watch Company, and develop it with them. "Our long-term aim," Ike says, "is to design and build our own movements, but it will take us a few years to get there." The Tourbillon's movement is a first step in this direction, as it was developed jointly between Ikepod and the manufacturers. This insistence on the technical quality of the watches, not just their appearance, is one element that distinguishes Ikepod from a competitor such as Franck Muller. As one commentator remarked, "If Franck Muller watches are art for the wrist, then Ikepods are modern art for the wrist." This is true if the styling is all that is being compared. But Ikepod also invest in the mechanical quality of their watches. Some have also compared Newson's designs to the work of Alain Silberstein, the French 'architecte horloger' who borrows elements from modernist and Bauhaus design to decorate the hands and dials of his watches:

Manatee Watch,
2001

Seaslug Watch,
1993

Newson's vision, however, subsumes the stylistic into the whole.

—   This insistence on authenticity is a key part of their strategy, and a concern that Newson and Ike share. Their first watch, the Seaslug, is an automatic mechanical diving watch that uses an ETA 2893-2 certified chronometer movement. The brightly colored ribbed bracelets are in natural rubber (steel and leather bracelets are also available). The choice of colors (black, orange or green) like the choice of faces (silver, black or anthracite) are not just about style but also about visibility. The Hemipode collection uses a similar family of bracelets, while the movement is based on an ETA 7750 caliber movement. The case is a monocoque design that can be opened from above, and the watch also has an off-center window opening on the rear to reveal the movement. The Megapode collection is a watch developed for pilots that incorporates the American ASA flight computer. This uses two logarithmic scales that can be operated to calculate fuel consumption, and distances and to convert units. The start and stop buttons for the chronograph are placed on the left-hand side of the dial, unconventionally: this makes for a more balanced design and allows a pilot to access them more easily, as a pilot wears the watch on the right hand.

—   The two most recent additions to the Ikepod collection are the Tourbillon and the Manatee. The latter is inside a square case instead of the circular ones used on the other watches. The watch has an inner bezel with world time zones marked on it—an unusual and efficient solution to the challenge of creating a world time watch. The Tourbillon has a 'sans heures' face overlaid with a classic Newson pattern, and a small opening within the face that reveals the tourbillon movement. The combination of minimalism and technology sets it apart from other high-precision watches, and underscores Ikepod's unusual and creative strategy in a market dominated by tradition.

2/5   Design details for
the Manatee and
Tourbillon Watches

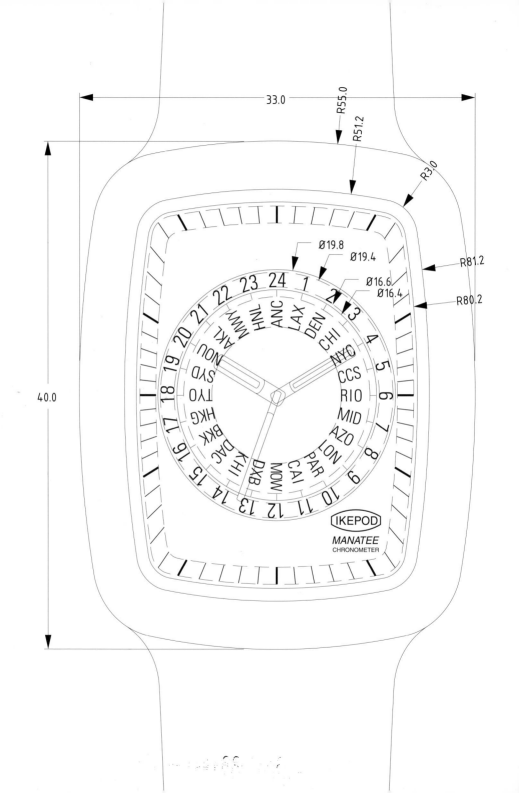

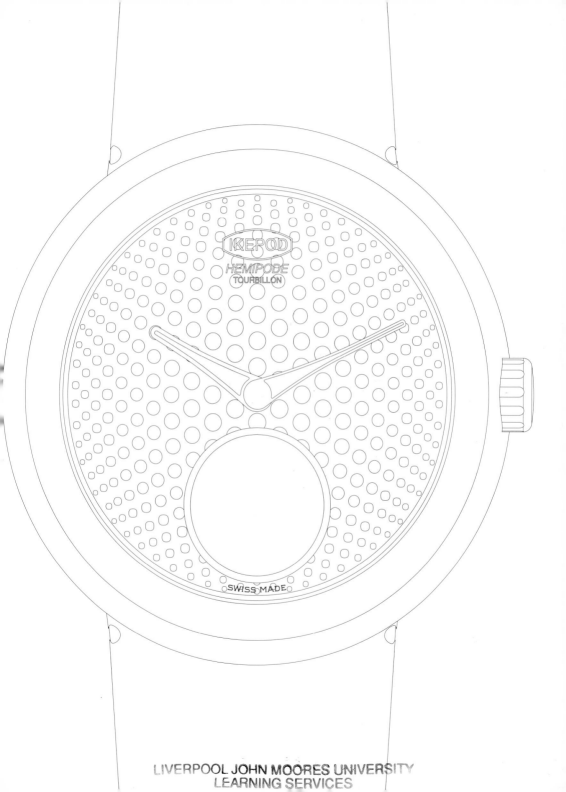

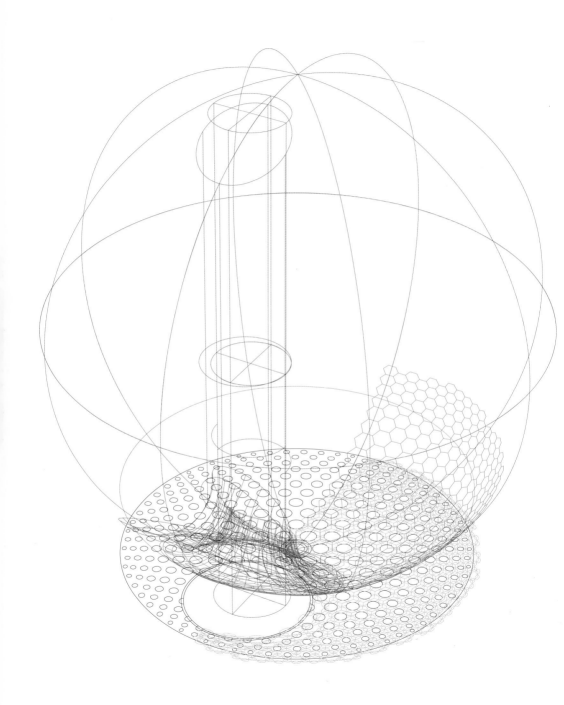

Vidal Sassoon

Vidal Sassoon
Hairdryer, 2001

—   Oxford University in the mid-
1960s, and you could tell the American girl exchange students at
once: as soon as they got to England they'd rush down to London
and get their hair cut in the approved five point bob shape by Vidal
Sassoon. Thirty years later, when Marc Newson decided he should
cut his waist-length ponytail (part of the "designer as rock star"
image he had had affixed to him by the lifestyle press) it was
Sassoon to whom he turned. Newson had met Sassoon through
a mutual friend, who knew that Sassoon was looking to redesign
the range of products marketed under his name by Procter &
Gamble. Sassoon and his wife Ronnie visited Newson at his office
in London, and they chose Newson as the designer for the task.

—   What Sassoon achieved when
he opened his first salon in London in the late 1950s was to make
hair styles modern, relying on cut rather than the old-fashioned
bouffant look. Famous clients flocked to him—notably Mia
Farrow, who had a Sassoon cut for her role in Roman Polanski's
film 'Rosemary's Baby'. Success built on success: Sassoon is
now an international name, and has been for a long time. Most
people in their seventies are thinking about retirement rather than
rebuilding a business. But Sassoon has sponsored the London
Fashion Week for the last few years, and, with his wife, still keeps
actively in touch with his twenty-six salons and thirteen schools of
hairdressing around the world. Two young, new stylists, Peter Gray
and Eugene Souleiman, are in charge of maintaining the creative
edge of the business. "Only youth has the true sense of today,"
Sassoon has commented. "You've got to look at the youth and try
to understand the way they are feeling and thinking. If you don't,
you're old-fashioned. It's as simple as that."

—   Newson recognized Sassoon
as "one of the innovators who were ahead of their time." He has
described his approach to designing for Sassoon as "going back
to the simplicity of the early Sassoon look." There are two ranges
of styling products, one for individual consumers and one for the
professional market. "For the consumer range our main concern
was delivering real quality, and so a real improvement over what is
on the market." The hairdryer and two different curling tongs came
to the market in early 2001, with the professional range to follow.
"The professional range," Newson explains, "is not just for use in
Sassoon's professional salons but for all professional salons as
well. We did a lot of work on developing these in terms of
ergonomics and performance, an important question when you
think a professional stylist may be using a hairdryer for several
hours a day. There are a lot of issues involved and we've learned a
lot from Vidal and his colleagues."

/9   Packaging and
       Hairdryer, 2001

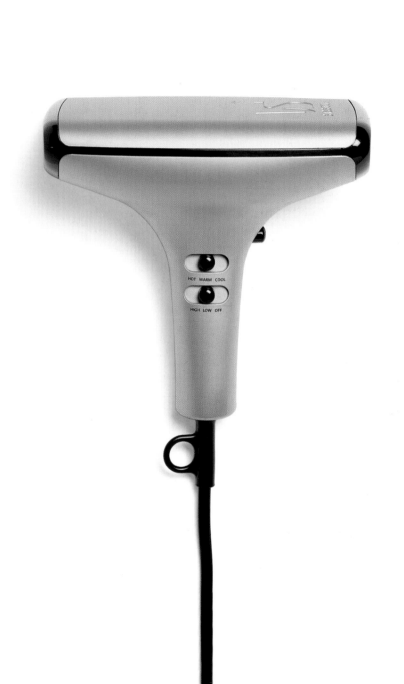

Marc Newson
— Starting Here

—

The Sassoon project also represented a quantitative move forward for Newson and his team. For the first time they were working for a major international client, Procter & Gamble, on a range of products for industrial serial manufacturing. The change of scale validates the concept Newson formed with Benjamin de Haan in 1995. The Sassoon range is the first series of industrial products to come to market from this process; others, with equally powerful international companies as clients such as Nike and Ideal Standard, are in the pipeline.

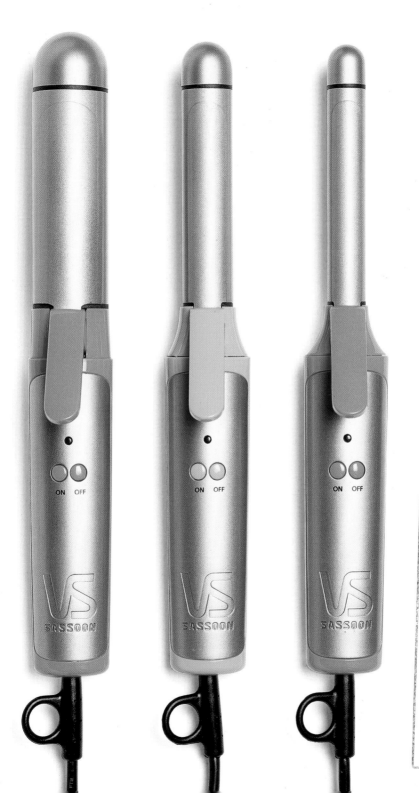

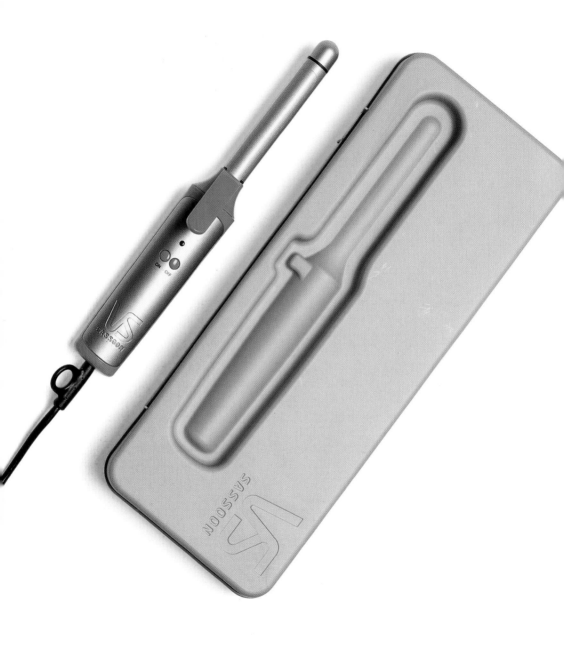

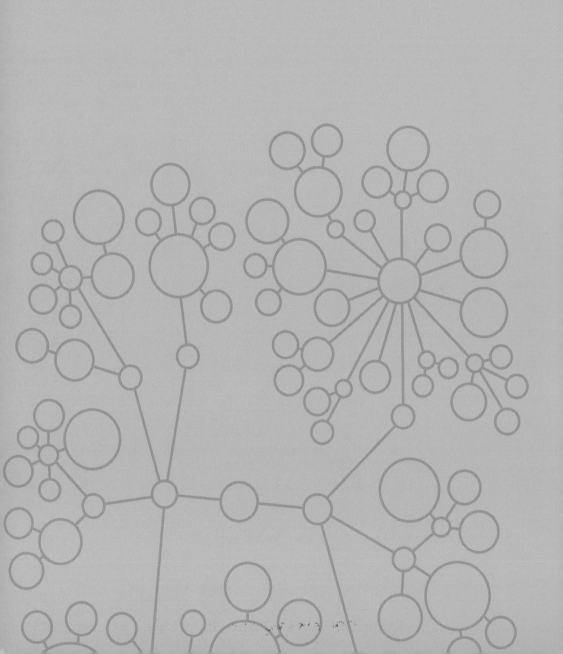

—   Walk into Marc Newson's office in London: it's a large white room with three large windows on the street side and single lamps hanging from twelve bosses in the elaborate plasterwork ceiling. Walls and ceiling are painted white: files sit in large white box frames along the walls. Desks and tables and the floor are white, gray and green, chairs black. A few objects on top of the frame cabinets. On one a huge Shiseido perfume bottle (one of his first high-revenue commissions in Japan), then the Ricard jug, a Gello Table (the last two reminders of his time in Paris), a Coast Chair, and finally a three-foot-high model of a Space Shuttle ready for launch, booster rockets in place. Is this a time line? Newson has often said he'd like to design a space station. The colors on the occasional objects are bold, accentuated by the monochrome setting. His own office is small, behind a door with a teenage-like sign "Danger: Marc's Room." On his desk are badges from NASA and Star City, and two of his Ikepod Hemipode watches. ("No," he says, "they're rip-offs from China: they cost ten bucks each over there." He seems amused at the idea his work is worth imitating.) And a millemetric double industrial calliper–box fresh. This is the object that sets the tone: exactness, order, concentration. The box frames in the main office are mounted on wheels, ready to roll. Poise and precision are the underlying themes of the office and, in some ways, of Newson's work, alongside the bold colors and exciting curved forms.

76/9   Marc Newson's
office in London

—   Newson has come a long way to get to London: from Sydney via Tokyo and Paris. His design work has moved from one-off pieces of furniture and bar interiors to contract production for chairs, lights, and display systems, and now to work for major corporations such as Procter & Gamble, Ford, and Nike, on projects ranging from car design to aircraft interiors to ranges of consumer goods and sportswear. Part of the purpose of this book is to chart that progress. Its other aim is to set Newson's own career against the development of the role of the product designer over the last three or four decades. The demand for Newson's services has not only grown with a wider appreciation of his developing talents, but also against a background of the growing appreciation in many kinds of businesses of the importance of design.

—   One can explain this growth in a number of ways: historically as the influence of the youth culture that began in the 1960s permeated visual culture generally, beginning with graphics; technologically in terms of the opportunities created by new materials and processes; economically with the response to developing new markets; in media terms as the spread of communications, especially television, heightened visual awareness; in corporate terms as a response to competition; in class terms as the degradation of social hierarchies allowed for more variation and expression; and even politically as a response to the end of the American cultural hegemony after Vietnam. The evolution of the meanings of the

Marc Newson
—　Getting There

80　Shiseido Perfume
　　Bottle, 1992

word "designer" shows this pattern of change. The job description that would today be "graphic designer" would have been "commercial artist" in the 1950s and early 1960s and even after that the word "designer" was normally used in a qualified way—fashion designer, aircraft designer, car designer and so on. This is reflected in the titling of two of the major books on design of the period, Raymond Loewy's 'Industrial Design' and Milton Glaser's 'Graphic Design'.

—　　　　　　　　　　　　The word "designer" and the design profession flourished in the design boom of the 1980s. Fueled in part by rampant capitalism in the United States of the Reagan era and in Thatcherite Britain, companies increasingly used design to win greater market share through advertising and packaging. They also realized that brands and logos had an important role in developing customer and stakeholder awareness and were therefore assets to be nurtured. The reorganization of government services and public monopolies in Europe created new identity design work as well as work for national and international clients during the same period. Development of this potential market for design was also aided by advances in computing, especially the Apple Mac personal computer and software programs such as Word, Photoshop, and Quark Express, which enabled a new professionalism in production directly from the designer's own office.

—　　　　　　　　　　　　Even after the worldwide recession that was the crowning achievement of Reagan/Thatcher economic policies, design retained its status, even though design companies were as hard hit as other businesses. Since then graphic design has grown into a major area of corporate activity, and many design firms have formed partnerships with marketing and communications companies, or developed a communications arm, to provide a wider range of management services. Martin Sorrell's worldwide WPP Group is an example of this: the group comprises advertising agencies, management consultants and design groups in an interlinked network.

—　　　　　　　　　　　　This development has promoted the role of the designer from supplying solely graphic solutions to playing an integral role in the development of a company or brand's personality, requiring interfacing with different aspects of management. It represents an extension of skills and responsibilities. This development has led to the formation of large design agencies, with a wide range of specialties, especially in communication via the Internet and worldwide web. The reasons for this development will concern us later; what is relevant here is that product design is following a similar path.

82/3　Storage unit in the
　　　London office

—   Product design was traditionally an in-house function: for every maverick like Raymond Loewy designing for Studebaker in the 1950s, for example, there were studios full of anonymous modelers at General Motors and Ford. Even the legendary Harley Earl, chief of design at GM, comes across today as more an executive than a designer, and he only worked in car design. Some progressive companies in the 1960s, such as Olivetti, outsourced product design to designers such as Ettore Sottsass and Mario Bellini, as did companies producing short-run specialized goods like porcelain and silver, furniture and lighting (for example Rosenthal, Kartell, Flos, and Cappellini, among many others). But outside Italy the independent product designer was something of a rarity, and the design world within Italy known only to the cognoscenti.

—   One of the factors that changed this perception, many commentators agree, was the appearance on the design scene of Philippe Starck. His energy, humor and inventiveness sent the lifestyle press scrambling for their tape recorders, eager to catch his wry and witty comments, delivered between mouthfuls of champagne from the bottle always by his work table. The Starck lemon squeezer became an iconic object, a must-have gift on wedding registries from Perugia to Peoria. Starck, in short, got the sort of media treatment reserved for fashion models and rock stars. Companies became famous for commissioning him: French electronics group Thomson asked him for a showroom design and instead he created a complete product range, and the mail-order company La Redoute asked him for a list of his favorite products and ended up publishing 'Good Goods', a forty-eight page catalogue of new products with Starck's own ethical branding. The message that Starck put across to the media was not just about himself and his work, but about wider issues in design and society. His ideas were vividly and forcefully expressed, and that they were dressed up in neat slogans ("Nous sommes Dieu" or "Tomorrow will be less" or "Moral market") did not mean that their content was invalid or irrelevant to Starck's work and position.

—   Starck's success with the media had two consequences. The first is that the media became interested in product and furniture design in general and in other designers. Or rather, that Starck accelerated a process of interest in design that was already underway, as design's role in everyday life became clearer to people (Terence Conran's pioneering work with Habitat in England and Monoprix in France is important in this respect, as is the work of Charles and Ray Eames in education and exhibitions in America). The second is that companies found that investing in product design and designers could be profitable, both in terms of the corporate image and the marketplace (again, there are precedents in graphic design and architecture, and in transport design). Here the nature of Starck's advocacy did play a role: if he had simply promoted himself without a wider, one might say political, stance on design he would not, for all his talent, have reached as wide a general audience.

—   Other designers, including Newson have been the beneficiaries of this process, and Newson's own career can be looked at in such a light. And his creativity has been compared to Starck's both in terms of the quality of design and his appeal to the media. Some have even talked of Newson as "the second Starck," but the assumption that there is some Darwinian process about design evolution or that there is a "top designer"–a Tiger Woods of the drawing board–is a wholly misplaced one. Newson is the first to admit that Starck has helped him: generally through his example and specifically through Starck's recommendation to the Italian lighting company Flos that they commission work from Newson. Starck's success in Japan, where his extraordinary buildings created an immediate market for the work of Western designers, was one factor in Newson's going to Tokyo at one point in his career, for example, though as he says "actually my family lived there at one time and I just loved Japan. And it was an obvious destination for an Australian."

—   But just as graphic design has moved from the drawing board into the boardroom, so product design has become not just a means of adding new products but also of creating or upgrading a company's image. Newson's work for the start-up company Biomega is a classic example of using design to position a new brand. But larger companies as well are now looking to product design as well as graphic design for this added dimension. A new corporate identity for a major company becomes a serious media event, as when early in 2001 the petroleum giant BP decided to jettison several decades of design equity in favor of a new mark and the strapline "beyond petroleum" (a line they were later to discard, claiming it was only created for the launch). When in the previous year Bob Ayling decided to step aside as chief executive of British Airways, one of the reasons he cited was the problems the company had faced over their new "World Images" identity system. More happily, in the product field, the Dutch electronics company Philips recently teamed up with Italian kitchenware specialists Alessi to upgrade their domestic electric goods, just as Thomson have maintained the Tim Thom team created by Starck, and Absolute Design in France and Jasper Morrison in Britain have been involved in designing new urban tramways. There are plenty of other examples of such new partnerships between design and manufacturing.

—   More than the talent of designers is driving this process. As markets become global, so the theory has it, then sourcing production becomes more generalized, and with increasing competition consumers become more discerning. Add to this the levels of regulation on products and services both nationally and transnationally, and the result is that what is offered by competing companies in the same marketplace is often very similar. An airline flight across the Atlantic, for example, is much the same whichever airline one chooses, taking the same time, offering broadly similar comfort and amenities, and often in the same make of airplane. Electrical goods such as dishwashers guarantee much the same quality and lifetime, whatever the make. Even fashion-conscious items such as sneakers have similar standards of construction and performance, whether by Reebok or Puma, Nike or Adidas (who recently commissioned a shoe from the Audi design team). To create and hold market share, companies are increasingly investing in their brands, and adding design-led products to reinforce the brand message. Seen in this way, design becomes the differentiator between broadly similar products and acts as the company's cutting edge in the marketplace. And in this role product designers are not only being called on to create forms, but to innovate total concepts.

— In the last few years Marc Newson's work has moved into this new area, with projects for major corporations as well as for individual clients. Benjamin de Haan describes this new role for product design as "the third leg," meaning that design now sits alongside production and marketing as essential supports for a company in a competitive martketplace. In the change from industrial to post-industrial capitalism, industry reinvented the production and technical aspects of manufacturing in the 1970s and 1980s, and in the 1990s the financial aspects. After that, as de Haan puts it, "companies woke up to the value of design, and the fact that it costs the same to do a job poorly as to do it well." And de Haan is one of the reasons why Newson is better able to tackle this new range of challenges. De Haan studied engineering, art and architecture at Cooper Union in New York, worked with PDD making patent prototypes, and specialized in computer-aided design systems for modelmaking while working for the architect I.M. Pei's New York office and later with Airbus Industrie in France. When he met Newson in Paris in 1996 he suggested that he put his computing skills at Newson's service, since "we were both mechanics and techno geeks, Marc with analog experience, mine being digital."

— The two formed Marc Newson Ltd. This enabled Newson to extend his workload without losing detailed control of each project. He now works with a small team of experts, using their computer skills to visualize his ideas, rather than with his own hands as he did for so many years, starting in his grandfather's workshop in Sydney when he was a child. "I see the computer as a virtual workshop," he explains. "Until a decade or so ago I used to have a real workshop and really enjoyed that, but I realized that my strength lies not in making things but in conceptualizing them and developing them. Equally I don't want to run an office full of designers drawing up the things I've sketched on napkins and handed over to them! But you have to know how to do it, so as to design things more efficiently, and so as to tell others how to complete the design, and more importantly, so that when you come to meet the client's people, you can command total respect."

Ford 021C

—   If the path linking intention, execution and reception of a design project were a straight one, composed of clear logical links, then writing about design would be much easier—and much less interesting either to read or write. For a successful design project bonds a whole range of different ambitions and viewpoints, and it is this synthesis, and the resulting range of new perspectives it uncovers, that makes for its interest and success. The concept car that Newson designed for Ford is a good example of this.

—   J Mays was appointed vice-president for design at Ford Motor Company in 1997. He had previously worked for Audi, on the design of the TT roadster. Then, as a freelance designer in California he had created the Volkswagen Concept 1, the precursor of the new Beetle. He jokes that he first sought out Newson because he wanted a discount on one of his Ikepod watches. "Seriously, though, the watches are one of his most iconic pieces, absolutely perfect and pure in their balance of shape and technology. You could say that Newson's work was influenced by '2001', by NASA, and by everything going on in the space program in the 1960s and 1970s, but I think it's astonishing that he's managed to take that material that looks straightforward but is in fact very amorphic and geometrically complex, and make a personal design language out of it, which is then applied across a whole range of products. It's very rare to find a young designer whose work isn't a take on someone else's language."

—   Newson recalls that Mays got in touch with him after getting a note congratulating him on his appointment at Ford. Their initial discussions were about products that Newson might design for Ford. "The idea of a concept car design," according to Benjamin de Haan, "kind of grew out of these discussions: it was never a formal agenda." And as Newson says "the furthest thing from our minds when we started discussions was that I might design a car." Mays recalls that his first thought was to have Newson work on an interior design: "I thought that based on his chairs and furniture he could probably come up with a design DNA for the entire interior of a vehicle." Sketches and projects and a few visits later, and the idea of a whole vehicle, based on a next generation Fiesta chassis and engine, came up. "His first sketches scared me a little bit, quite frankly, because they looked so naïve, and the first computer-generated images scared me a lot more, because they were really out of proportion. It was basically a problem of scale." From there the project passed, according to Mays, through three stages, starting with an initial small scale project "which sat on the corner of my desk for about six months while I thought about it." Then both Newson, on computer, and Mays, using his specialist team at Ghia in Turin, did further development work ("we took half the car each," Mays observes, "and the reality is there was probably a middle ground there where we learned stuff off his computer-generated imagery

and he also learned quite a lot about lines and highlighting and how shapes transition on an automobile") before finally deciding to build a complete concept car. A concept car is primarily a means of expressing where the values of the company are going, either through showcasing an important new technology, such as a mixed-fuel engine, or a lifestyle application. As a positioning statement a concept car is first directed to the company's clients and customers, and the world in general through the press, but it also has an internal message, to the company's employees, about the direction the company intends to take. It is in these terms that the radicalism of Newson's design needs to be understood.

—   Given that he currently drives an Aston Martin DB4, and a Lamborghini Miura, and has owned such classics as a Jaguar Mark 2, Citroën DS and Sunbeam Alpine, Marc Newson admits that he always wanted to design a car, so the invitation from Ford was very welcome. "But there was no formal brief," Newson points out, beyond using an existing platform. "However," he says, "I wanted to create something relevant, and at the back of my mind was the possibility that such a car might be built, so it was designed to be buildable within the existing technologies; there's quite enough unbuildable design in the industry already."

—   "Car design is very self-referential," Newson says, "like a number of other areas of specialized design! So car designers tend to focus only on car design." Ford employs several thousand design staffs in sixteen locations worldwide, and Newson first went to one of these, in Irvine, California, to get a handle on the techniques of car design, such as designing in clay, a material he had not used before on such a scale. Similarly, as Frank Gibney, Jr., has pointed out, there was a new vocabulary to learn: "terms such as beltline (the line that runs around the midriff), A-pillar, greenhouse (the cabin top), and tumblehome (the angle at which the roof meets the windows). He also suggests "there was tension with other designers, who wondered how an outsider warranted his own car and so much attention from the new boss." Mays concurs: "A lot of my time was spent keeping my other designers away from Newson, so he could work in his own way." So for the final phase of the design Newson moved to the Ghia studio in Turin, where he worked continuously for eight months to prepare the car for its launch at the 1999 Tokyo Motor Show, where it promptly won the accolade of Best Car in Show.

—   Mays feels that while product design, graphic design and fashion seem to live happily together and share concepts and ideas, car design sits to the side. One of his aims at Ford is to "extend the design DNA of the company," and so involving an outside designer, with no car industry experience, fitted in with this approach even if it was never a deliberate strategy. Mays' own analysis of Newson's design is mainly in terms of its formal qualities. "If you look at my own car designs," he says, "you'll see that they use three lines at most.

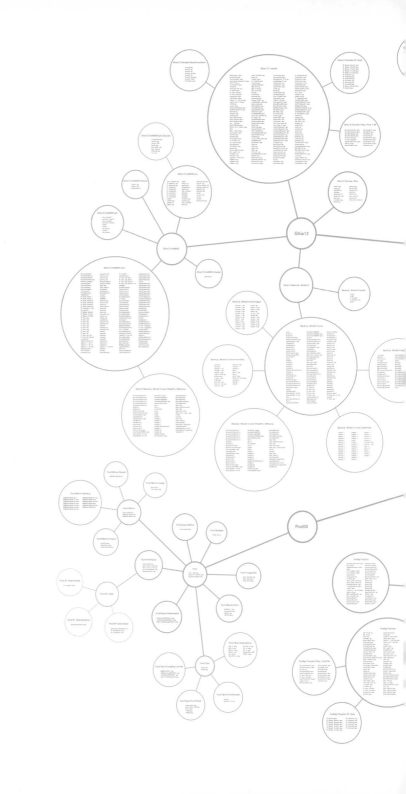

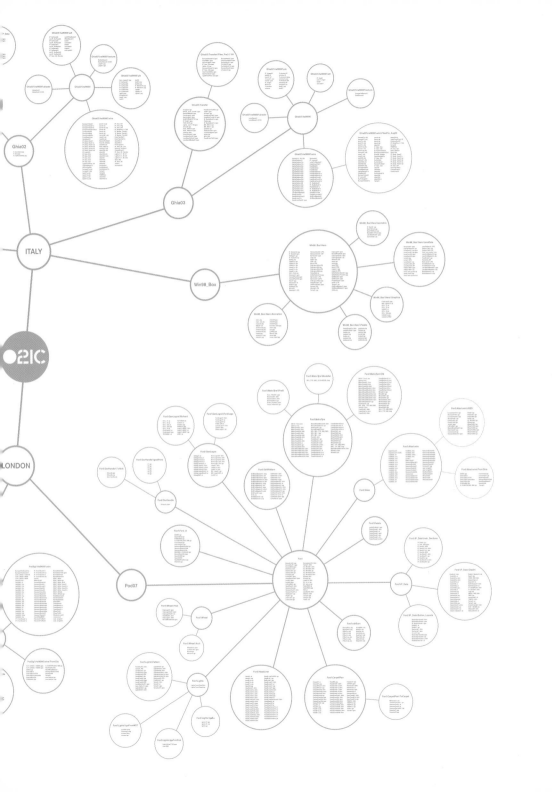

I think that kind of rigor is needed in modern car design, because when you get down to that minimal situation, you have to think hard about design and how to make it work. Newson had this incredibly pure idea of this simple tube that runs from one end of the car to the other: a motif you find in some of his chair and interior designs as well. The solution was a rectangle with accelerating and de-accelerating radii, and a lot of the development work was about scaling this up to the right size. Here the problem is that a curve that looks fine on a quarter-scale model cannot be simply enlarged and look the same full-size. One of the reasons why we split the design task into two after the model was to explore this scaling-up process, on the computer screen for Newson and, initially, in clay with my people in Turin. What we learned together was that you need to cheat slightly, to adjust the absolute parameters to get the full-scale appearance you want. That's what I brought to the party, but I knew that Newson's own design rigor would ensure that the project would work."

—   Mays knew from the start that Newson's design was going to be unconventional, not that he had any problem with that. Nor did the audience of teenagers at the Tokyo launch, who found the bright orange object enthralling. American critics were less enthused: one termed it "a style statement, not a car." This leaves unanswered the question of which cars in the last fifty years have not been style statements, of course. Other critics used the term "retro," a term recently also applied to the Citroën 2CV, as if it had been designed in the 1930s (which in fact it was). Another compared the design to the British 1950s Hillman Minx, a feat of memory if not of relevance. As Mays wrote in the promotional blurb for the car, "If you don't get it, don't worry, you're probably not meant to." It was the fixed attitudes, and fixed vocabulary, of the motor journalists he had in mind, and their reaction, while not uniformly hostile, still validates Mays' concern that car design operates in its own, enclosed world. As Newson comments, "We were expecting to be panned by the automotive press but most of them liked it."

—   It is in this sense that Newson's own description of the car as "a car for people who don't like cars" should be understood. "It's a town car," Newson explains, "because it had to be something relevant, both from a functional and cultural point of view. So I wanted it to appeal to people who were not car people, but who had a broader frame of reference, that were interested in popular culture, interested in music, interested in film. People to whom cars don't mean that much, who just see them as a way of getting from point A to point B. And above all, something to make people smile, to show we don't take ourselves too seriously. I wasn't trying to reinvent the wheel, but I wanted it to look like a car, not a grounded Starfighter—nor a bread bin either!"

—   Fun the car might be, but it's serious fun. Mays calls the car "more George Jetson than Georg Jensen," and it's true that Noddy or Fred Flintstone would feel completely at home with it. But simple doesn't mean unsubtle.

Creating the formal and smooth elegance of the main outer shape was a complex process of development and learning. One way this smoothness was achieved was through dropping conventional headlights and taillights and replacing them at the front and rear with panels of light-emitting diodes (LEDs), programmed via a ROM chip to act as indicators, brake lamps, and sidelights. LEDs react faster than incandescent lamps to an electrical input, so this innovation not only enables the design solution, it also makes the vehicle safer, since warnings, especially at speed, are given sooner. This element alone shows how the concept is not simply stylistic but an integrated work.

—   But it was the interior that was the real challenge. "What I primarily wanted to do," Newson explains, "was to clean up the interior, and get rid of all the nasty intersections, and collisions between surfaces that you see on a lot of cars." Traditionally interior design had been a teamwork process—or rather different elements (seating, dashboard, trim) were handled by different teams. The result is very often a collection of compromises, within which the driver and passengers have very little choice. One starting point of Newson's solution, in practical terms, was to improve the driver and passenger's situation. So, for example, the floor is completely flat, and meets the side walls in a gentle curve. The roof and outer-door pillars are thin, so as to increase the amount of incoming light (there is no central pillar between front and rear doors), and the rake of the windshield and rear window is slight. Minimizing the internal geography in this way at once creates a more spacious and less cluttered interior. To enable easier access, the front doors open forward, the rear ones backward: Newson uses a clam-shell system for this that reduces the footprint of the vehicle with doors open.

—   The seating has a further innovation: the front seats swivel through 90 degrees outward so that getting in and out is simply easier. The pedestal-mounted front seats can be adjusted for height and rake, to suit the driver and passenger. In addition, the whole steering column and dashboard can be adjusted vertically to suit the driver, who can also adjust the twin instrument dials in the dash to the desired angle using a joystick. These ergonomic solutions are in fact quite subversive within the traditional canons of car design. The car used to be seen as a personal motion capsule—a cockpit not a cabin. Newson proposes the car as a transitional space, whose function is as much about stopping as moving, carrying as well as transporting. (This idea is heightened by the treatment of the trunk: it has a conventional hinged lid but will also pull out as a tray to allow for easier loading.) The radicalism of this approach also comes through in the controls. As Newson says, "You only need a few controls to operate a car, and I wanted to remind people of this simple fact." Four of these controls are the buttons on the steering wheel, to control the automatic transmission, a technology derived from motor racing, but used here to make the driver's life easier.

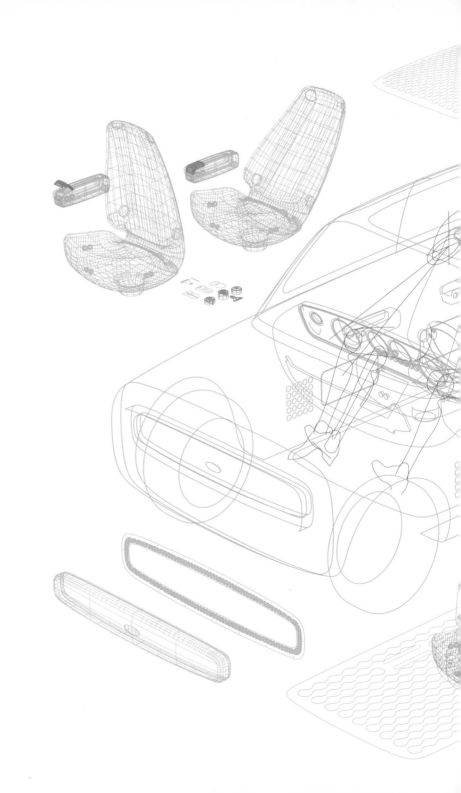

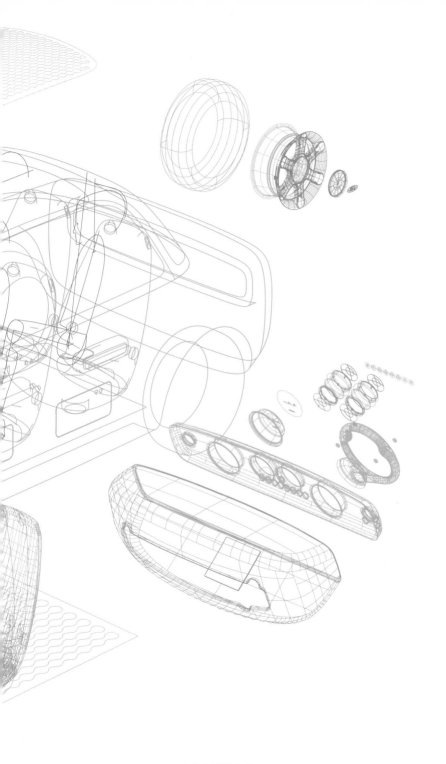

— "The interior represented well over fifty percent of the work on the car," Newson points out, explaining that "a car isn't just one product, it's more like cramming five hundred products into one space." A very tight space as well: the car is smaller than any other car Ford has in production being about four inches shorter than the Ka. It's a measure of the success of the design that the finished vehicle seems so roomy and well-proportioned. Of course, there are signs of Newson's other work all over the car: the instrument dials are created by his watch company Ikepod, the steering wheel is a reminder of his hook for Alessi or the earlier Komed light, the seats are upholstered by B&B Italia, for whom he designed the IO table, and the colors—orange and silver and white—used on the exterior and interior of the Tokyo car echo the bold tones of his furniture design. The carpet uses a Newson pattern, and the tires were specially made by Pirelli to Newson's design, including the profile and the tread. When the car was shown at the Milan Furniture Fair the Prada subsidiary Miu Miu designed a special set of luggage for the trunk—and Fendi made a pair of white fuzzy dice for the windshield.

— To read the car as a self-referential collage of Newson motifs—down to the Orgone patterns in the carpet—is to miss the boldness of the concept as a whole. "I wanted to create something relevant," Newson says, "but not just from a functional point of view but culturally as well." If the result of this carefully integrated work is culture shock for some viewers, that reveals the isolation of some standpoints. And the concept cars (a second, in green—Newson's next favorite color after orange, as he once said—was also built and shown in 2001 at the Design Museum in London) not only had cultural work to do in the wide world but within Ford itself. "At one point," Mays says, "we had a pretty nice little car sitting there, albeit a pretty odd-looking car: its simplicity and toylike graphic nature were really quite shocking—and part of its appeal. The next big step I had, which could have been a potential hurdle, was to tell Jacques Nasser, the CEO of Ford, that I was going to show this thing with a Ford blue oval on it at a motor show. So I flew Marc into Detroit one evening and we went out for dinner with Nasser. For whatever reason—maybe because Jacques is Australian as well—they hit it off really well. We showed him the car and he thought it was hilarious. We told him we were going to paint the car orange, and were trying to brainstorm names for it. Jacques suggested we called it after the Pantone color number of the orange, 021C. That's how the name came about—we only realized later that you could read it as 21st century. That was quite cool." What Mays was trying to do with the concept car was to get away from the style-obsessed design previously prevalent at Ford and "to show in a non-threatening way to the rest of the organization what a simple design exercise could have by way of impact. The project was as much about internally changing the way we thought about design as well as changing the way the general public saw Ford as a company. To signal to both the internal and external world that we're a lot more innovative than the rustbelt personality some

106/7　Interior details
on the 021C

perceive." For as Stephen Bayley has pointed out, Ford has made the decision "to evolve from being a reliable, but mundane, provider of blue-collar cars to being a design-led world-class manufacturer with a boggling portfolio of products."

—   For Newson the car project was one of the most complex and demanding he has ever undertaken, and the tsunami of surprise and delight the 021C has generated validates the intense effort involved. "My only regret," he says, "is that I never drove it. I was going to as soon as it was finished, but that day I had to leave Turin for Tokyo to set up the launch: they had to drag me out of the 'carrozeria' before I could get a chance to try out the car! The point is that it is a fully functioning car, not simply a design study that wasn't feasible. It had an engine, it drove. Most of our time was spent working within these parameters."

8   The 021C exhibited
       at the 2000 Detroit
       Motor Show

9   Sumo wrestler in
       the 021C

0/11   The green version
       of the 021C in a
       special display by
       Imagination at the
       Design Museum,
       London

O21C

—   It was the kind of project a designer might dream about but hardly ever expect to get: "Please design my private aircraft for me." And not just any aircraft: a triple-engined, transoceanic jet, the Dassault Falcon 900B was the object. Dassault's own suggested finish for their business jet included walnut veneers and comfy rugs—a sub-sonic Victorian parlor. Newson's client wanted the project to be "the coolest thing ever." Newson, who had been fascinated by real and model aircraft since his childhood, was delighted with the invitation: "My $40 million toy," as he called it to Alice Rawsthorn. Silver, black and green dominate the interior design, which is wholly contemporary: the exterior is covered in a pattern of circles of increasing density as it sweeps to the tail. But this is not just decoration: the designer started with a bare fuselage, and had to devise the seating plan, select and modify or redesign the seats, plan and design the finishes and lighting, as well as choose the colors. To make a strong and original statement in such a small space is a considerable achievement.

Design for interior
fuselage pattern,
Newlines, 2001

—   If the interiors of most passenger aircraft seem to be the same, whatever the livery of the company flying them, it's all Walter Dorwin Teague's fault. In 1955 Boeing invited the distinguished American designer to advise them on the interior appearance and fittings of their new long-haul multi-passenger jet, the Boeing 707. Teague stipulated a half-a-million dollar fee, which in the heady economy of the time Boeing accepted. And he made a condition: he would show them the design when he was ready, but no work in progress. This Boeing also accepted. Teague and his assistant Frank del Giudice then built a full-size mock-up of the complete cabin on a site near their offices in New York, and set to work. They found new plastic wallcovering materials that could be applied to the aluminum skin of the interiors, used recessed light fittings behind diffusing plastic, and developed high-backed contoured chairs: the standard elements of aircraft interior design to this day. Teague's team also developed seating systems, customer service units and methods for operating galleys and service trolleys. These were tested using groups of "passengers", until the final version was shown to Boeing's executives on a simulated full-scale "flight" from Washington to Seattle, complete with engine noise, inflight food, and even scenery projected onto the windows.

/17   The Falcon 900B
Jet, before and
after Newson's
work on it, 1999
Final exterior livery
by Richard Allan

—   Teague's fee was well earned, in that he provided Boeing not only with a design but an operating system. Teague was also very proud of the job, and kept inviting visitors to "come and see my new airplane," to the annoyance of the Boeing engineers who had designed it (by adapting a design from a military refueling aircraft). His system, among other things, promoted the air hostess to her role as the face of the aircraft and airline—previously the captain or chief pilot would have welcomed passengers aboard. Teague's work set a standard that has not been varied, until now, with the arrival of the Newlines concept.

18   Main cabin interior
      on the Falcon
      900B

19   The after cabin
      as seating or
      bedroom area

— Quite simply, Newlines is the first new idea in transatlantic air travel since the arrival of the wide-bodied jet. And when one thinks that the jumbo jet came over the horizon in the 1970s, it is surprising that the idea has not come around before. Julian Cook, corporate finance specialist at Chase Manhattan In New York, had worked for a time with regional airlines in South America, and remembered how they operated business-class only services with planes carrying forty to fifty passengers. Why not, he thought, create a similar service on the busiest business route in the world, between London and New York?

— The figures are in his favor: the Civil Aviation Authority estimated in 1999 that there are four million passenger journeys across the Atlantic each year, of which one third are in business class. With a target customer base of over a million, a small operation would not have to build a large market share to be profitable. An eighty-seat aircraft, for example, could undercut the main airlines and still operate profitably. Cook estimates the price of a return flight as being around $3,000 on his airline, as opposed to $5,000 from a major carrier. "In May 1999," Cook explains, "I realized that there was a huge gap growing between business class and economy both in terms of price and comfort. And even if you did opt for business class, did you really want to share a plane with four hundred other passengers. Business class inside the plane might be comfortable, and is if anything becoming more comfortable at the expense of economy, but the travel experience also includes embarking and disembarking, and I remembered from South America just how relaxing it was to fly in smaller groups. Today across the Atlantic your business seat is great, but getting to and from that seat is the hassle. So our original idea was to create something more efficient, quicker and more affordable for the business traveler."

— Cook selected the Boeing 757 as the ideal aircraft: it has a long and proven flight record, and its nominal two-hundred-and-twenty passenger capacity could be reconfigured to accommodate eighty reclinable seats. "At this point in preparing the business plan I realized that competing on price alone was not sufficient. We would be vulnerable to price-cutting, and so it would be better to create something that had more value, that people might aspire to, and want to use rather than just save money by using. Then I thought about what has happened in the hotel market in recent years, with the development of boutique hotels, and how they had used design to create a distinctive product."

— Cook recalled an article he had seen in 'Wallpaper' magazine about Newson's Falcon jet: "I remembered it really clearly as it was the first time I'd seen the interior of a corporate jet that looked really different. Most of the time they are finished in beige or mahogany. There are a few designers and companies working on jet interiors, but it's normally very corporate or very traditional—or all in gold if it's for some Arab prince! So on my next trip to London I arranged to see Marc:

20 Cabin interior for
the Newlines
Boeing 757

21 Alternative designs
for the cabin walls

all I had was a couple of pages of the business plan and an interior diagram of the aircraft, but he agreed to work on it."

— Newson and Cook agreed that Newson would oversee all the design aspects, and they brought in the London-based agency Farrow Design to work on the graphic aspects such as signage and menus. The final livery will be designed by Newson: at the time of writing these details have not been decided, but some of the preliminary design ideas are shown here, and the book jacket and section openers are based on patterns Newson designed for the interior. Farrow Design also did the graphic design for this book.

— Newson found rapidly, but not unexpectedly, that working on a commercial aircraft had considerably more constraints than working on a private jet. "Designing a private jet is both more open-ended as to budget, and less regulated," Newson comments, "but commercial aircraft are strictly controlled, and we have a fixed budget to work to, of which the costs of the seats themselves is a major part. Seats used to have to be designed to withstand a nine-gee impact, but this has been raised to sixteen gee. So designing and developing a complete seat is out of the question, both in terms of time and money. So we are using an existing, certified seat frame unit, and redesigning the total shape, both the upholstery and the electronic gear, such as DVD players, screens and telephones, that go into it: an exercise in biomechanics as much as furniture. And as I spend a lot of my time in airline seats I certainly intend it to be comfortable: I get the impression that a lot of the people who design plane seats don't do a lot of flying."

— Though—as with many of Newson's projects—there was never a very detailed design brief, Cook felt it important that the cabin should feel like a united space. "The subdivision of cabins in large jets is really colonial thinking, setting up imperial barriers. We wanted the whole interior space to be for all the passengers, so there are no hierarchies in the design—not that it will be monotonous either." Or as Newson puts it,"Most of my work was for the interior, and was very challenging and complicated. But I think the final result will nonetheless look different and be part of the image of the new airline." Following the tragic events of September 11th, 2001, the Newlines project is on hold. Whatever the outcome, the project shows how important the creative role of design can and must be in creating the personality of a new product.

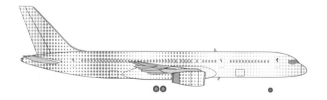

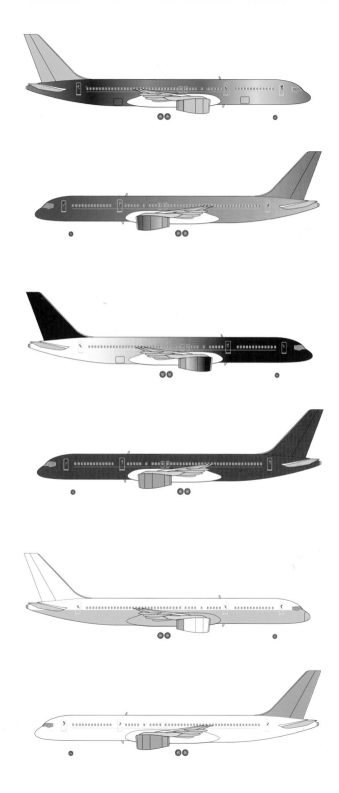

126   Prototype cutlery by Alessi for the Lever House Restaurant, 2001

—
Lever House and the Seagram Building sit on opposite corners of New York's Park Avenue. They symbolize a key moment in America's corporate hegemony (even though the two corporations that built them were respectively British and Canadian in origin). They are landmarks in America's postwar economic and political triumphs, and their architectural form asserts the victory of the Modern style in architecture, a process recounted with wicked glee in Tom Wolfe's book 'Bauhaus to Our House'. The Seagram Building was designed by Mies van der Rohe and opened in 1958, while Lever House, by Gordon Bunshaft of Skidmore Owings and Merrill, was completed six years earlier, in 1952. The recessed position of each building on its site, so creating a public space in front of the building, had an immediate effect on later zoning and planning laws, and their stark facades, finished in steel and glass—blue glass for Lever, bronzed steel for Seagram ("whisky and washing-up liquid" as one irreverent critic put it—became a model for corporate headquarters buildings for a quarter of a century.

—
The Seagram Building interiors were designed by Philip Johnson, at that time a passionate modernist. He also designed the Four Seasons restaurant in the building (and lunched there very often). The building has a second restaurant in the basement, the Brasserie, recently redesigned by New York architects Diller and Scofidio for Restaurant Associates and their chef Luc Dimnet. The restaurant has won several awards for its design.

—
Lever House is currently being refurbished (with Skidmore Owings and Merrill as consulting architects). The refurbishment includes a restaurant: Marc Newson is designing it, to open in Spring 2002. "It's going to be pretty high-end, because of the location and the fact it's in a prestigious building. I'm doing everything, from the toilets to the cutlery (which is being made by Alessi specifically for the restaurant). And Emeco are making the chairs I've designed for it as well. It's the biggest budget interior I've done so far."

—
As Newson says, "I've been trying to wind down from doing interiors. I don't enjoy designing interiors as much as I do designing products. There are infinitely more constraints. And working with subcontractors of different quality means an interior becomes like the only prototype you ever build. With products you can build several prototypes and work out all the bugs, then decide what to actually make. With an interior you only have the one possibility. But with the Lever House, apart from the fact that I was working for clients I'd worked with before, I felt the project was so important I couldn't turn it down. And unlike some of the other interiors I've done, this one will potentially be there for a long time. It would be nice if it stayed in place for a while, even became some sort of institution. It's by far the most ambitious architectural project I've undertaken."

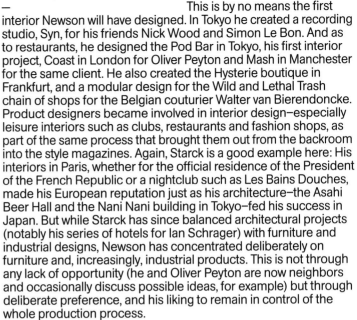

— This is by no means the first interior Newson will have designed. In Tokyo he created a recording studio, Syn, for his friends Nick Wood and Simon Le Bon. And as to restaurants, he designed the Pod Bar in Tokyo, his first interior project, Coast in London for Oliver Peyton and Mash in Manchester for the same client. He also created the Hysterie boutique in Frankfurt, and a modular design for the Wild and Lethal Trash chain of shops for the Belgian couturier Walter van Bierendoncke. Product designers became involved in interior design—especially leisure interiors such as clubs, restaurants and fashion shops, as part of the same process that brought them out from the backroom into the style magazines. Again, Starck is a good example here: His interiors in Paris, whether for the official residence of the President of the French Republic or a nightclub such as Les Bains Douches, made his European reputation just as his architecture—the Asahi Beer Hall and the Nani Nani building in Tokyo—fed his success in Japan. But while Starck has since balanced architectural projects (notably his series of hotels for Ian Schrager) with furniture and industrial designs, Newson has concentrated deliberately on furniture and, increasingly, industrial products. This is not through any lack of opportunity (he and Oliver Peyton are now neighbors and occasionally discuss possible ideas, for example) but through deliberate preference, and his liking to remain in control of the whole production process.

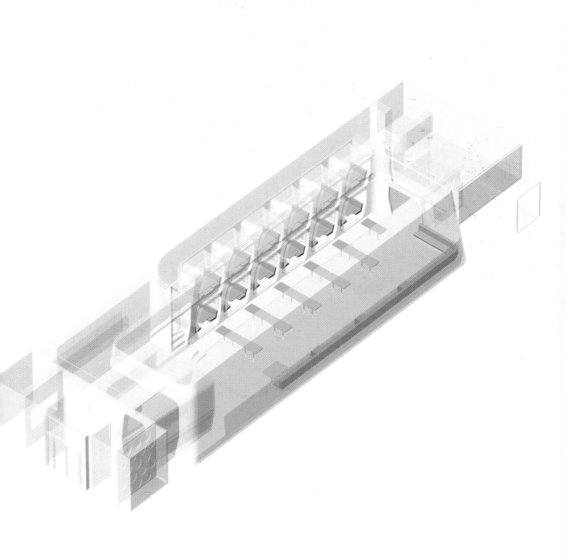

—   The first book about a
designer's work is a milestone of some importance, and the
book 'Marc Newson', published by Booth Clibborn Editions in
1997 and designed by Richard Allan and Nicolas Register, is
no exception. It's a stunning celebration of Newson's work, in a
lavish horizontal format, with a long introductory essay by Alice
Rawsthorn followed by visual studies of the work to date with
Newson's own wry comments. This is an approach to an
introductory book on a designer that is familiar and correct,
despite the attempts of publishers and authors over the years to
find alternative square holes for this round plug of the designer
monograph. The secret is to use the formula to enrich or subvert
the reader's expectations–or, ideally, do both.

—   Such books necessarily have
a celebratory quality, since they are about both achievement to
date and promise for the future. What each book chooses to
celebrate and how the celebrations are orchestrated is often
more interesting than the fact of celebration itself. So it is in this
case. Alice Rawsthorn's text narrates Newson's childhood, time at
art school and life in Sydney, Japan, Paris, and London through a
series of anecdotes, which are often told in Newson's own words,
vivid and entertaining. The reader gets a sense of the problems
facing a young and often penniless designer, who manages
nonetheless to have a great deal of fun, and produce some
extraordinary work. Talent and charm–and a fair share of luck–spill
out of the narrative in a highly seductive way: his girlfriend in Tokyo
shares an umbrella with someone who turns out to be the head of
a design furniture company, he "borrows" enough material from a
model-mosque-builder to complete the Pod of Drawers (later
bought by Jean-Paul Gaultier), a commission for a perfume bottle
allows him to buy his dream car, an Aston Martin–and find out
about forming aluminium during the hunt. Newson called this part
of his life "the Artful Dodger phase," and no wonder.

—   Within this wholly engaging
structure Rawsthorn positions Newson as a solitary, independent
creator, driven by his own vision of things. This certainly fits with
the way he still works today, as a single "creative" with a small group
of technicians rather than delegating or sharing projects with a team
of other designers. The average design studio, if there is such a
thing, is normally organized on a leader and team basis, that is to
say there are one, two or three main designers (often the partners
in a small studio) who head teams made up of other staff on each
project. The degree to which the lead designer controls the project
is as much a matter of temperament as anything else, though
training plays its part. Design history, as it is taught in Europe and
America, is strongly influenced by the Modern movement, and
by the definitions of the designer laid down by Gropius and his
colleagues at the Bauhaus. This view of the designer as a social
catalyst is perhaps best enshrined in Nikolaus Pevsner's 'Pioneers
of Modern Design' (although Pevsner, trained as an art historian,

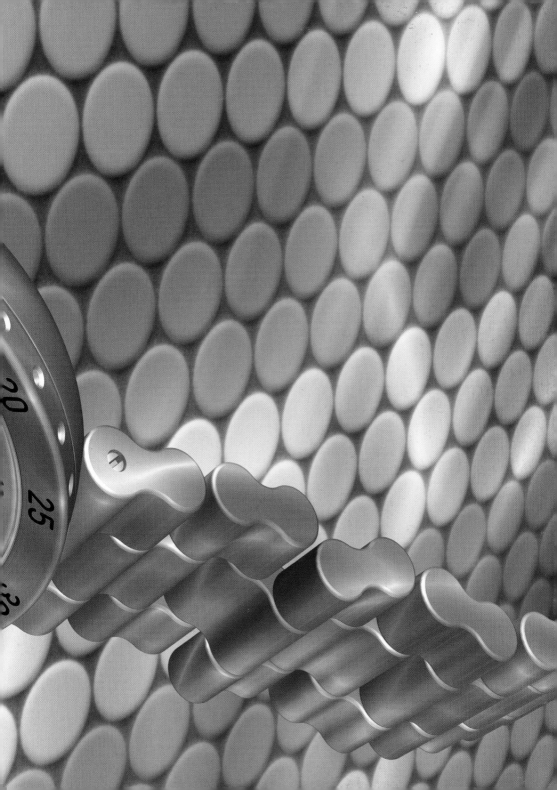

Marc Newson
—   Getting There

—   Ford 021C
—   Newlines
— · Lever House Restaurant
—   Marc Newson Book

uses an art-historical model of the evolution of design). From this
the concept of the designer as "problem-solver" emerges, and
it is an attitude toward design with which many contemporary
designers agree, positioning the designer as in some way
society's guide, leader and friend, and motivated by a social and
even political agenda as much as by a pure creative vision.

—   Rawsthorn offers a slightly
different analogy. She defines Newson more as one would an artist
as someone moved to create beautiful and significant forms.
She cites the influence of late eighteenth- and nineteenth-century
painting on Newson–for example Jacques Louis David's 'Portrait
of Madame Recamier' in relation to the Lockheed Lounge chair,
and the opulent settings of late-nineteenth-century interiors to
Newson's love of materials. In addition, the designers whose work
she cites as influencing Newson, such as the Castiglionis and
Bruno Munari, are those designers whom one would categorize
are most individual or "artistic." Philippe Starck, another very
original designer, but who has a loudly proclaimed social agenda,
albeit a highly individual one, is discussed more in terms of his
personal help to Newson, and his influence on the perception
of designers by manufacturers and the public. Describing
Newson as an artist seems to me to be apt, in particular in using
the nineteenth century as a context.

—   The interesting question is
whether the traditional distinction between artist and designer
is still relevant. Art historians sometimes try to place artists as
being creatively independent, though within an artistic tradition,
and also exercising a sort of visual leadership, in which the view
of society they offer to the world is both mirror and spyglass.
The claim to artistic independence, at least until the start of the
twentieth century, has always seemed to me to be based on a
Romantic analysis of the role of the artist, rather than a social or
economic one. And as to the question of visual leadership, there
is little doubt that artists now share this with other creative people
such as designers and filmmakers, or may even have surrendered
it completely to them.

—   The visual treatment of
Newson's work in the book supports the themes of the text.
The digital handling of the images, by Allan and Register often
places the work in an abstract space, unsupported by, or, rather,
freed from gravity, either floating in white space or against a
uniform colored background. Such is the technical control of
these images that the occasional actual photographs look
strangely unreal in comparison, an unfortunate intrusion into
the pure formal environment in which Newson's work hovers.
This placing of the work is not just about technical virtuosity,
however. It mirrors the degree of painstaking detail that Newson
puts into his own work, it celebrates the change in his working
style from physical modeling to computer-based design, including
the use of Pro-Engineer among other computer programs, and it
announces Newson's freedom from the historical and formal

43 Arthur C. Clarke
in 2001 with a copy
of the 1999 Marc
Newson book

constraints of design tradition, a factor that gives his work its individuality and appeal.

— The visualisation process at times goes further: the Seaslug watch is placed as if underwater, in an aquarium with a Newson-designed pattern to its base, for example. The Orgone stretch lounge and the Alufelt chair are both shown as cut-outs, but their polished surfaces reflect a tropical poolscape, with palm trees and azure sky: "pure David Hockney," as Newson comments. It's a brief and improbable moment of fantasy, a sudden irruption of luxury and lifestyle. And a reminder, in its surreal way, that Newson's work does engage with the world, is for use and has a purpose. Text and images balance in presenting a portrait of Newson innovation and creativity. When a friend showed Arthur C. Clarke the book on Newson, his comment was "I wish we'd had him to design the sets for '2001'." "Great, I was five years old at the time," is Newson's comment on the compliment.

44/45 Interior spread,
image created by
Richard Allan and
Nicolas Register

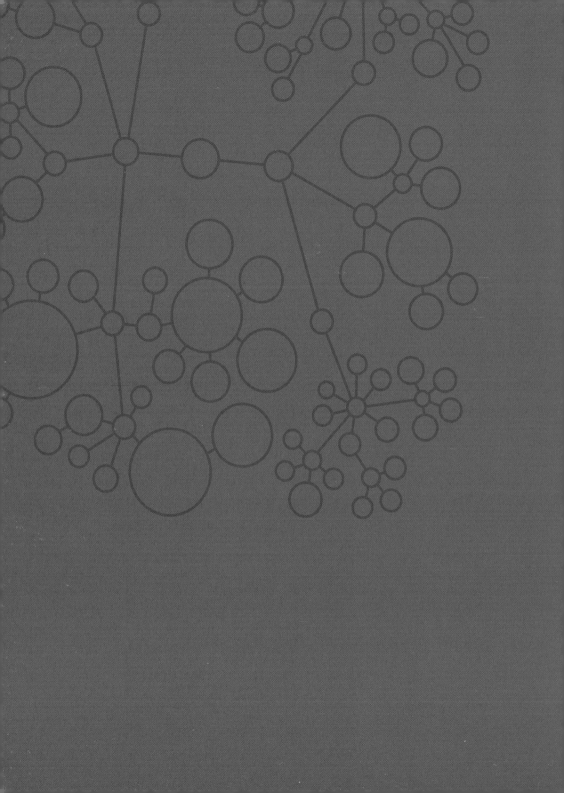

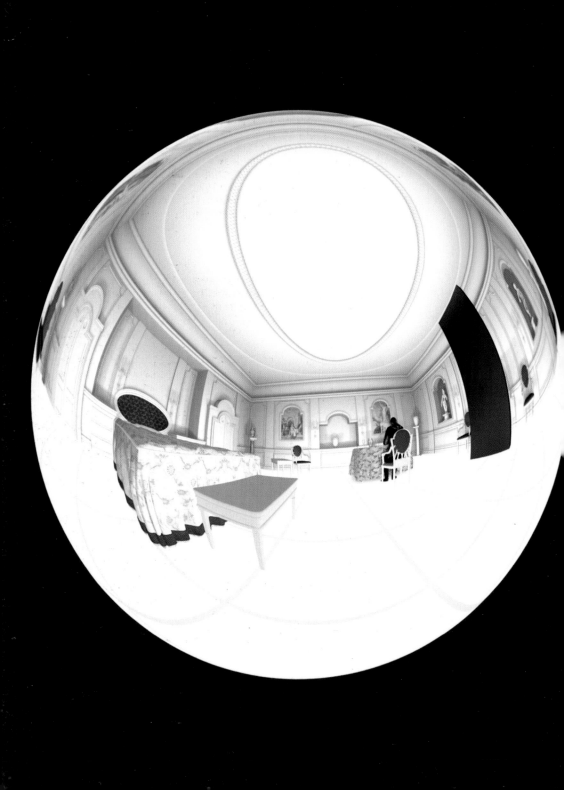

—   Stanley Kubrick's 1968 film
'2001: A Space Odyssey' was a commercial and cult success
from the start. Five years in production and with special effects
that were not to be matched until the digital revolution some thirty
years later, the film is both an astonishing visual statement about
the future and a set of parables about evolution and its limitations,
society and technology, human and artificial intelligence. The film
can be read as a pure visual experience (the final sequence in
itself earning it the accolade of "the Ultimate Trip"), or as a serious
attempt to explore what contact with an alien civilization might
mean. Arthur C. Clarke, on whose short story "The Sentinel" the
film was based, and who co-wrote the screenplay with Kubrick,
once said that "if anyone understands the film completely, then
we've failed."

—   One thing a formal analysis
of the film and its development suggests is that is expressly a
visual film, or rather a silent film. The dialogue in the film is
completely formal, leading to no deepening of personal contact,
and that interpersonal relations have no role in the scheme of
things the film presents. (In this way the film is a logical successor
to Kubrick's earlier Cold War comedy, 'Dr Strangelove or: How
I Learned to Stop Worrying and Love the Bomb'.) Interestingly, an
early version of the script included a voice-over explaining the
state of world relations (the Nuclear Club) when the main
contemporary action starts, which was later dropped, and the
original plan for a continuous original musical score was shelved
in favor of using classical music (Strauss's 'Blue Danube' and 'Also
Sprach Zarathustra' for example) as the background–rather in the
manner of the way pre-sound movies would have an extempore
musical accompaniment. By depriving the viewer of either social
information or narrative musical cues to the action, the open-
ended nature of the questions the film raises is emphasized.

—   '2001' is one of the films that
journalists have often cited as having an influence on Marc
Newson's work, and some commentators have assumed this
to mean that he simply borrowed a visual language from the
film. Certainly Tony Masters' set designs provide a wealth of
inspirations, and a determined iconographist could forge a
link between some of Newson's early furniture and the Olivier
Morgue Djinn chairs that are used on-screen in the space station
sequence. But forgery Newson's work is not, any more than
Kubrick's masterpiece was only a visual romp.

—   Another series of film Newson
has in the past mentioned to journalists as influential are the early
James Bond movies made by Cubby Broccoli and starring Sean
Connery. These are also Cold War techno-fictions, not rendered
more plausible by the substitution of a malevolent Blofeld (or other
omnipotent but cultured bad guys) for the tactical arm of the KGB
(SMERSH) in the original novels. And plausibility is stretched still

48   The final scene
        of '2001' re-created
        digitally by
        Nicolas Register

further by the array of weapons and gadgets furnished to the suave Commander Bond (Royal Navy) by "Q", a refined version of the mad professor who has been a staple of the film and comic business's gallery of characters ever since Dr. Frankenstein.

— One variant on the professor theme, however, is the character of Professor Peabody, in the 1950s Eagle comics featuring Dan Dare, captain of the British Spacefleet, where "the Prof" is a woman (and about the only female character in the whole series). Given the limited role of women in British science in the 1950s, Peabody is even more improbable than a British Spacefleet, just as the Bond author Ian Fleming's wartime service in the Directorate of Naval Intelligence suggests a triumph of hope over experience in the character of James Bond. But what links all three visions of the future–Dan Dare, '2001' and James Bond–is their potential of optimism and sense of fantasy. And these are the qualities that Newson reacted to. The imagery of the films suggested a world that he was interested in exploring: the films provided not visual models but coherent statements of possibilities. This is made clearer if one considers two other films that Newson himself cites: Andrei Tarkovsky's 'Solaris' (1972) and John Carpenter's 'Dark Star' (1968/9).

150/51 Prototyping the Event Horizon Table, 1992

— Tarkovsky's film is based on a novel by Stanislaw Lem: it describes the plight of three scientists whose station moves over the surface of a planet consisting entirely of an unfathomable ocean—unfathomable in the sense that the question of whether, how and why the ocean is sentient has not been resolved by decades of research and theory, and for which the evidence is physically and psychologically traumatic. 'Solaris', Lem writes, "is a symphony in geometry, but we lack the ears to hear it… a dilemma that we are not equipped to solve." Like 2001, but in a bleaker and darker format, 'Solaris' questions the definitions and limitations of our sense of humanity and belief in knowledge: nothing could be further from a visual crib.

— John Carpenter's 'Dark Star' is another matter: it's where ennui meets anarchy. Made in Carpenter's final year at film school at the University of Southern California, and later extended for cinema release, it tells the story of the fate of a lost ship on a futile mission (to discover habitable planets and destroy them). The crew of misfits–psychotics, surfers, hippies and a deep-frozen captain–are helped out by a computer that talks Descartes to the sentient bombs the ship carries (an early example of the "intelligent weapon," with predictable consequences). Black comedy with a poetic heart, the visual stance of 'Dark Star' can be seen in later films such as 'Silent Running' and 'Bladerunner'. The immediate appeal of Carpenter's film is its exuberance: the fate of the "heroes" of all three films, Kelvin in 'Solaris', Bowman in '2001' and Talby in 'Dark Star' is that they embark through apparent failure on a personal quest at the end. But to read this into Newson's own work too far would be exaggerated (despite the fact that his own desk-top computer uses Hal's voice to announce incoming messages!).

But it is perhaps not too far-fetched to say that Newson's feeling that he was empowered to explore such future possibilities was in part due to his physical distance from the world of European design. In the case of furniture design in Europe in the postwar period (and also before the Second World War) designers were in part conditioned by the Modernist debate about form and function, and the selection of appropriate materials and means to the purposes at hand. Modernism created a context in which the vocabulary of design was enormously extended and revised, and that context provided the setting for a large number of beautiful and persuasive objects, for which the Mies van de Rohe Barcelona chair can perhaps stand as a totem. But that context, by its very nature, both excluded certain considerations (color is perhaps the most evident example) and set in place a dialectic approach in which the justification of a design solution could not be simply visual or aesthetic but had to be grounded in a philosophical or political attitude.

Postwar European design shares something of this mind-set, even if not subscribing to the whole apparatus of prewar Modernism. So the history of furniture design in the 1950s and even up to Memphis can be read not only in formal terms of space, form and content, but also in terms of an evolving dialogue with industrial processes and materials and through that an ongoing analysis of society's place in an industrial culture. In particular, Italian design can be analyzed in terms of a reaction to the fake classical models imposed by Fascism and an interaction with new technologies, especially in plastics. Ettore Sottsass, for example, often defined his design position in wholly political terms, not that that reduces at all the formal beauty of much of his early work. (In this sense the work done by Memphis can be seen as finally freeing Italian design from the limitations of this intellectual context.) In the field of product design, Dieter Rams' minimalist solutions for Braun in Germany are not only elegant in themselves, but are eloquent of a redefinition of the social role of design in a new culture avid to distance itself from part of its history. A generation later in Europe, and elements in Philippe Starck's early work, such as the Cyrillic lettering in Les Bains Douches or the back of the truncated bourgeois armchair Richard III can be read as gestures whose content is as much political as formal.

What Newson brought to design, in these terms, was not simply the visual inspiration of Bond and Kubrick unattenuated by the political nuances of the European situation, but beyond that an involvement with popular culture (represented in part by commercial films) or rather an awareness that popular culture could be communicated and shared even through the language of formal design. There is a point of comparison here with British pop art, which in the hands of Eduardo Paolozzi and Richard Hamilton generated a new artistic language from American popular culture, through a process of contrast and collage. American pop art, for example in the work of Ray Lichtenstein or Claes Oldenburg, preferred to present popular imagery or objects in new media, a similar kind of social criticism but with a less-developed language. Newson did not simply adopt or adapt images from popular culture, rather he used the colors and forms of popular culture as a starting point in developing his own design language.

—   The use of bold colors in his work, for example, can be related directly–and superficially–to the surfer culture among which he grew up, and to which he paid homage with his 1988 Embryo chair, which was covered in bright wetsuit fabric. The use of curved forms can also be seen in the Kubrick sets, as has been mentioned: it also relates to the design of civil airliners, whence the title of the Lockheed Lounge. But the main reason for his enthusiasm for such motifs was their fantasy and optimism, something that was shared by the culture of Australia at the time. "This material was valuable for me," Newson says, "as a way of moving on, as a means of catapulting myself into something new. It wasn't something in itself, rather it suggested such things can be done. For me it represented something very optimistic, it showed the future. Today the future doesn't seem to be represented in such an optimistic way. Then it was, after all, the period when Concorde was built and man walked on the moon. And since then the most exciting things visually in cinema have been films like 'Alien' and 'Bladerunner', which take a much darker view of the future."

—   To make the surfer/sci-fi lifestyle connections for Newson is not difficult. After all, he did model clothes on the catwalk for Comme les Garçons, he had the coolest pigtail in contemporary history, and he had, and has, immense personal charm, wit and enthusiasm. To assume that Newson's design begins and stops there is wholly simplistic. Rather, what Newson surfs is the zeitgeist. He has an almost uncanny understanding of the present and so creates the forms that will resonate with that vision. It is not that he ignores the past or is ignorant about it—not at all—simply that the past does not have the same relevance to him. We tend to assume that to understand "now" we have to know "then" and make some structural sense of it. For Newson, "then" is not a scaffolding but a springboard.

152/53 Embryo Chair,
         1988

154/55 Lockheed Lounge,
         1986

—   The traditional, Western tendency is to equate the value of knowledge with its vertical, historical character, its depth. In this paradigm what might be termed "horizontal" knowledge is considered inferior, as it lacks the logical structures that are thought to underpin vertical knowledge. Horizontal knowledge must be shallow, as it were. In fact it need be nothing of the kind: it is simply differently structured from vertical knowledge, and can have as much, and as valid, a content. The clash between the aboriginal people of Australia and the first white settlers could be described in terms of such a clash of knowledges, as well as of cultures and of technologies. What we are seeing today is the increasing validation of horizontal

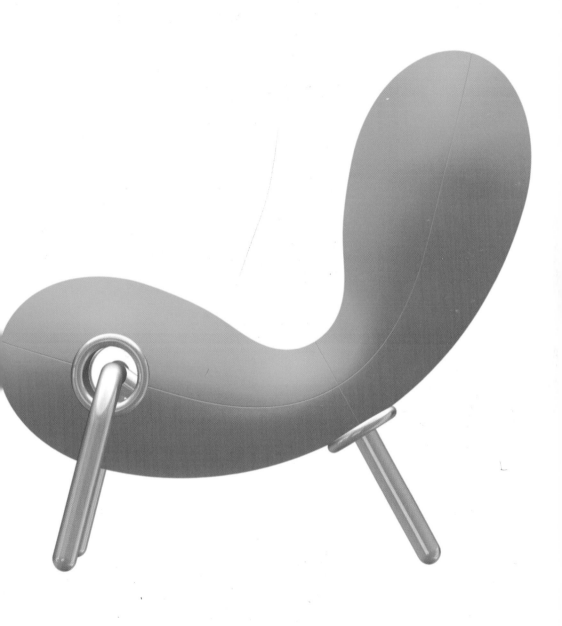

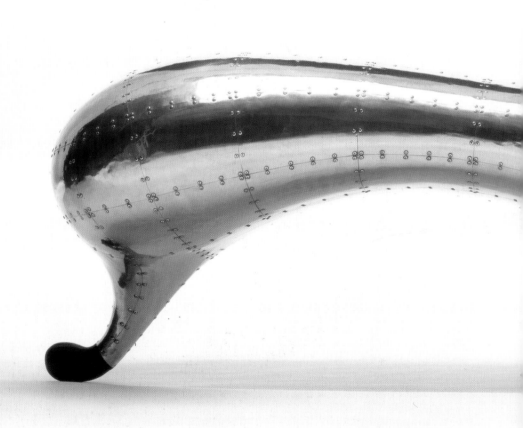

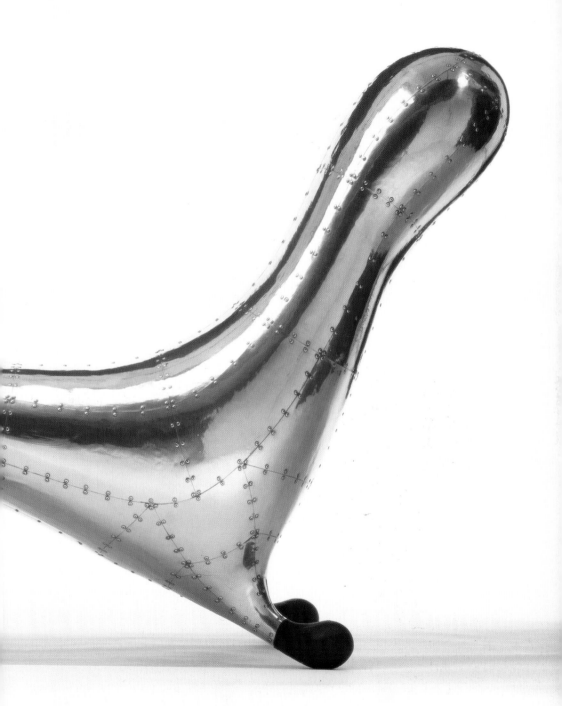

Marc Newson
—   Looking Good

157   Prototype of the
       Event Horizon
       Table

knowledge. Doctors may not know Latin and Greek but they do know genetics and nanotechnology. Contemporary communication systems, such as the web, also prioritize horizontal knowledge, which prefers density to profundity. Popular culture is a similar horizontal system, which, in part, inspires Marc Newson to create works of subtle form and stunning elegance.

—   Different designers use different modalities to arrive at their preferred solutions. The Dutch group Droog Design, for example, create subtle exercises in the minimal use of materials, be it felt for a bed or aviation-class carbonfiber for a chair. Jasper Morrison, a good friend of Newson for all that their styles are different, claims that "design is not done with rules, but with intuition. Intuition never lies." Philippe Starck blends exquisite form with his highly personal political agenda, whether into a sofa a family can nest in or a set of garden gnomes. Ron Arad uses his sculptural training to prove that steel need never be straight. Ingo Maurer combines small-scale elements, often figurative, with brilliantly controlled light to create pieces that are as much sculptures as luminaires. For many designers design is about a dialogue with materials, or with the existing conventions of a particular typology, or a manner of making a social or aesthetic criticism. Newson's work, with its attention to form, its concern over surface, its preoccupation with color, can be read in such terms as well. But it seems to me that while Newson is aware of the past, such knowledge does not hobble his creativity, and that his forward-looking stance empowers his work to reach beyond the confines of pure design and touch wider and stronger sensibilities.

Marc Newson
  In Control

—   "I'm a control freak," Newson points out, "which means I like to stay in charge of every stage of the development and manufacturing of my designs." It does not mean that he plays the autocrat ("too many designers like that about already," he comments wryly). He is open to comments and suggestions: Mark Farrow points out that when working on the Newlines project for Newson he and his colleagues could come up with ideas "even if they were more in his remit than ours," and Newson would adopt with them if he liked them. Nicolas Register, who has worked with Newson since 1997, says that while Newson makes the final decisions he is willing to listen to ideas from other people in the studio. "Ultimately," he adds, "Marc is the main source of ideas though he takes contributions from the team on their merits." In preparing this book I spent quite some time discussing how the material should be organized with Newson, and found he displayed the same charm and application as I had seen in more formal interviews with him. Changes would seemingly drift into the plan as part of a wider conversation, seemingly informal but in fact purposeful and knowledgeable. The same sense of purpose drives forward the research that underlines his design work. This does not emerge simply from the endless sketchbooks that fill a shelf in his office, and have accompanied him on his travels. It is in fact informed by his endless interest in physical materials and construction techniques, and by a restless visual curiosity. Newson himself has often said that working with his assistants and with manufacturers, and with new processes and materials, has been a valuable learning process for him. The following survey of his earlier work may suggest a "Newson look" (and other commentators have noted the regular use of curved forms and bright colors). I do not see this work as an exercise in style but rather as a series of studies in solving individual problems, infused with a common intelligence and an increasing fund of knowledge and experience.

0   Marc Newson in
    the early 1990s

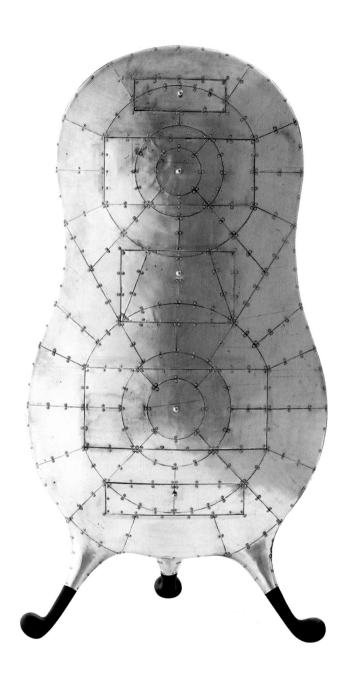

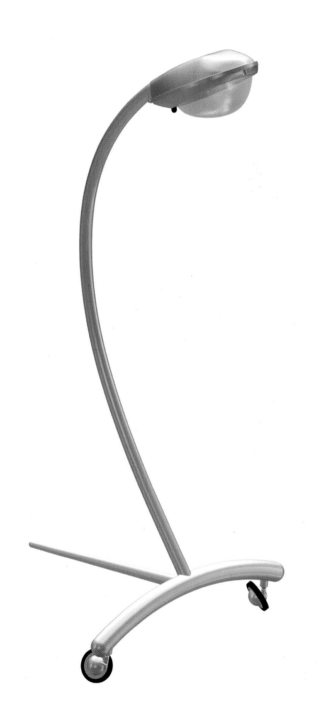

—   Starting work as a designer in Australia, he was his own designer, client and manufacturer, out o necessity. "It was what I had learned to do as a student," Newson points out, "and I studied jewelry so as to learn how to make things. His first pieces, exhibited at the Roslyn Oxley Gallery in Sydney in 1986, included the Cone Chair, made from sheets of aluminum, the Boat Chair, built of strips of wood molded together as in a boat's hull, and the Lockheed Lounge, whose name and metallic riveted exterior recalls the Lockheed airliners of the postwar perioc (A similar technique, of applying aluminium elements over a fluid fiberglass form was used in his 1987 Pod of Drawers. Pod was the name Newson used for his early independent productions.) The Lockheed Lounge was sold to an Australian gallery, but despite this accolade Newson realized that to achieve his ambitions as a designer he would have to travel. With his then girlfriend he went to Japan, where he met his first real client, Teruo Kurosaki of Idée.

—   "Working with Teruo was very informal," Newson recalls, "perhaps too informal sometimes. I loved Japan, as I'd often been there as a child, and it was visually and culturally a very exciting place to be and to work. Meeting Teruo was a real breakthrough, and he even paid me a regular amount, even though three-quarters of it went on rent! He had this ambition to become the leading producer of Western-designed furniture in Japan, with work by people like Starck. Before him, and contrary to what you might think, there was no tradition of making modern furniture in Japan. So getting the standard that I was used to, and wanted for my work, was very difficult, especially with the language barrier." Despite this Idée produced a version of the Embryo chair, covered in wetsuit fabric "one of the first pieces where I hit upon a discernible style," as Newson told Alice Rawsthorn. For Idée he also designed the Black Hole table ("made to my design by some Japanese surfers I met, out of carbon fiber") and the Wicker Chair and Lounge. His first lighting design, the Super Guppy lamp, was also edited by Kurosaki, using existing elements Newson found in a Japanese builder's suppliers.

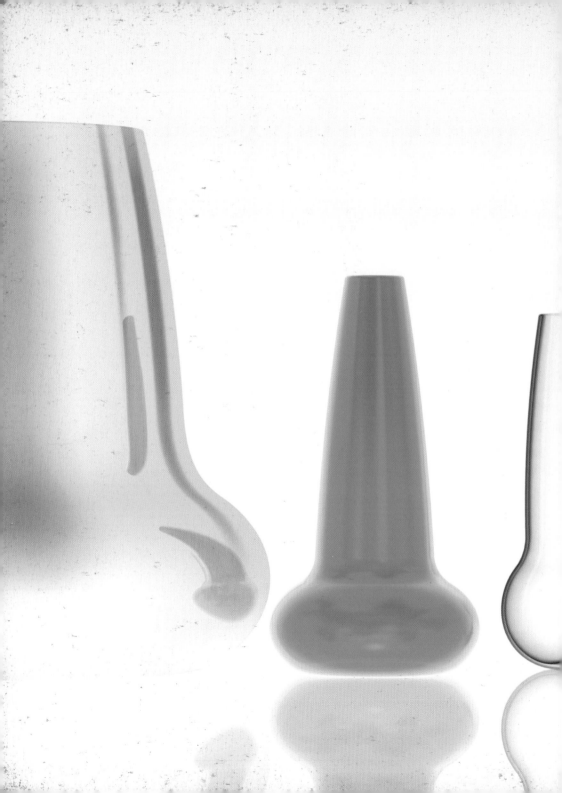

Marc Newson
— In Control

Cappellini was the first Italian manufacturer to edit Newson's work. At first they produced version of pieces that already existed. "Giulio Cappellini had seen my work in magazines and exhibitions, and he would say, 'I like that chair, can I produce it?' and I'd agree. Later he started commissioning pieces directly." Among the edited pieces were the Sine Chair and the Orgone Lounge, objects whose curved forms became icons of Newson's style. Cappellini also edited the Wood Chair that Newson had designed for a competition in Australia, using Tasmanian pine slats. The long Italian tradition of craftsmanship, and the postwar experience of the avante-garde manufacturers in working with new materials such as plastic, had both immediate advantages and some drawbacks for Newson.

— "In Italy," he points out, "for a long time there was no design training as such; everybody qualifie as an architect. As architects, they would give manufacturers visuall developed concepts to work from, and leave the manufacturers to finish the job. The result would have some of the manufacturer's design DNA in it as well. Everybody in Italy wants to be a designer and thinks they are designers, and that has been very valuable in building the industry, as you get standards of work which are unsurpassed. But if you're me, and want to control every detail, so the end product is my own DNA only, that can be difficult, and things can get a bit abrasive. Perhaps there's a difference of temperament, as well. When I was working with Ghia on the Ford car I had a hard time keeping their enthusiasm in the right place!"

— Newson also worked with the lighting company Flos, to whom he was introduced by Philippe Starck: in 1993 they edited his Helice Lamp. Other Italian clients included Moroso (TV Chair and Gluon Chair). More recently he has worked for Magis (Dish Doctor and Rock) and for Alessi. "Alessi take their time deciding on a project, but once they say yes they stick to my design," he points out, "so you don't have them trying to make changes because of what the marketing people think, which you sometimes get elsewhere in the world."

183   Mini Event Horizon
        Table, 1993

184/85 Aluminium
        Orgone and Alufelt
        Chairs, 1993

186/87 Strelka Chair
        by Magis, 1998

188/89 Helice Lamp, 1993,
        Torch, 1999

190/91 Soap Dish, 1997,
        Door Handle, 1999

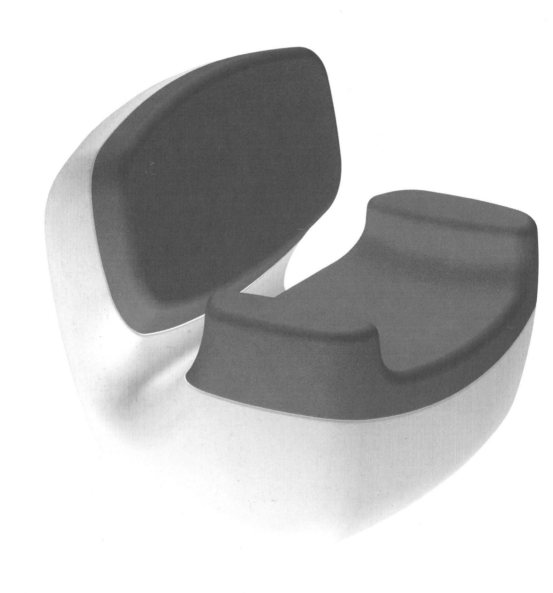

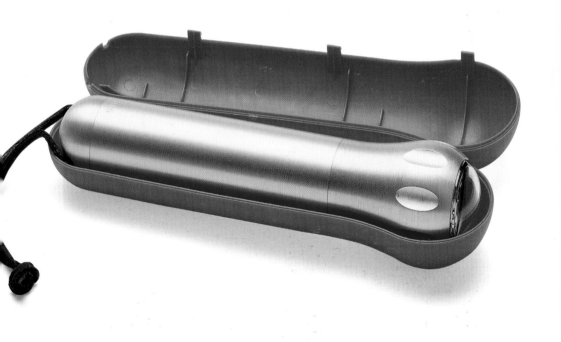

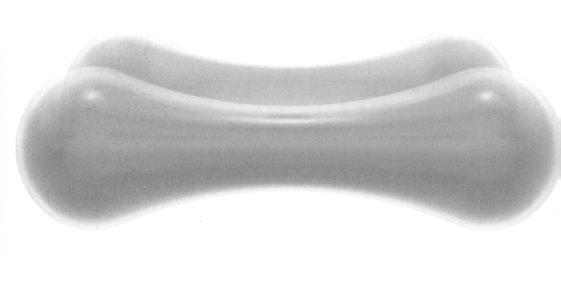

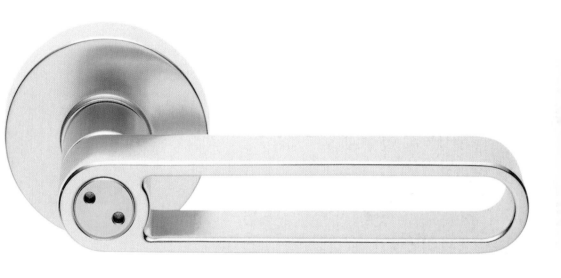

Marc Newson
— In Control

— Newson's decision to move to Paris cannot de described as part of a strategic design initiative. "I knew London already," he explains, citing the time he spent there when working for Idée, "and I didn't much like Milan—besides, I had a girlfriend in Paris." He found a studio in the red-light district near the rue Saint Denis, and worked there for his Italian clients and on new projects. "I didn't have many French clients," he says, "but then I don't have many English clients now I'm in London." The furniture designs that he created at the time—the Gluon, Alufelt, and TV Chairs and the Orgone Chair and Lounge, the Mini Event Horizon Table—were all for production by Italian companies.

— One local client, however, was the 3 Suisses mail-order company. Mail order has always been a successful merchandising method in France, in part because of the geographical spread of the population and in part because the mail-order companies themselves have moved their product ranges upscale as their client's disposable income increased (as compared to the UK, for example, where a larger proportion of the population is within a reasonable distance of quality retailers, and so where mail order has tended to remain a low-cost option). One 3 Suisses initiative was to commission original works from young designers. Andrée Putnam created one such design, Philippe Starck created his Ubu stool for them, and Marc Newson designed the Gello Table. This could be flat-packed for delivery, and came in three parts: a base, top, and a central toroid, all in plastic. The toroid unfolded like a paper Christmas tree decoration to make an openwork circular support between base and top. "For a temporary object," Newson explains, "it was slightly too expensive, so it didn't sell brilliantly. 3 Suisses insisted on finding someone to make it in France, which was probably a mistake as France was an expensive place to manufacture in at the time."

— Similar cost problems affected another French product, a water jug designed as a promotional item for bars and restaurants for the pastis-makers Ricard. Newson's intention was to integrate the handle and spout into the body, a sculptural solution that was too complex to mould economically in plastic. So it was finally manufactured in ceramic ("the project seemed to take forever, literally years," as Newson told Alice Rawsthorn). The French insistence on local production—and too often on local solutions—during the 1980s and early 1990s held back the development of design in France, at a time when, ironically, a different and more open attitude toward architecture was making France a center of built architectural excellence, with I.M. Pei's work on the renewal of the Louvre Museum, Gunndelson's on the Grande Arche at La Défense, Dominique Perrault's on the New National Library, and Jean Nouvel's on the Institut du Monde Arabe, and, outside Paris, Norman Foster on the Carré d'Art in Nîmes, Giepel and Michelin on CRAFT in Limoges and Nouvel on the Lyon Opera House.

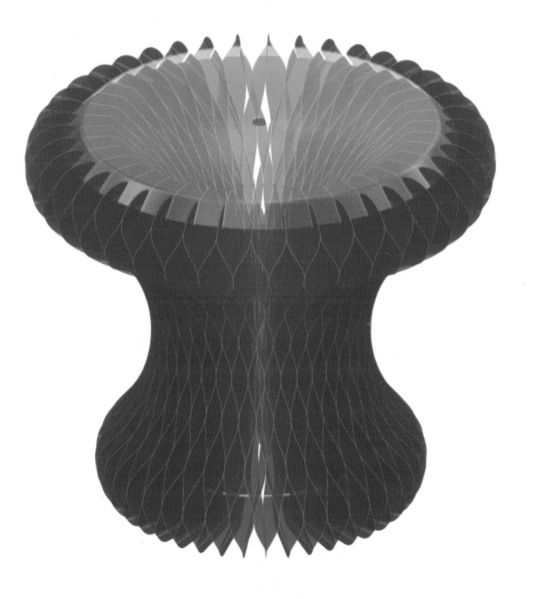

—   Another Nouvel building, the Cartier Foundation in Paris, was the setting for one of Newson's most successful events during his time in France. Hervé Chandés at the time the curator of the gallery space on the glass-walled ground floor of the Foundation, invited Newson to create a special installation as part of a three-man show. Newson created Bucky, a spherical open framework using uniform, modular, triangular elements in soft plastic with metal-linking elements. "I called it Bucky after the newly-discovered carbon molecule, the Buckminsterfullerene, which in turn got its name from the way the arrangement of atoms resembled the structures of his geodesic domes." This seems an appropriate homage to Fuller, who once named himself First Astronaut of Spaceship Earth.

—   "I kind of ran out of time on this project," Newson explains, "so didn't test the assembly in advance. Luckily Matthew Barney was having a show next door and came to help, and I had a Scottish friend living in Paris who'd worked in the North Sea oilfields, and he came along with a couple of ex-legionnaires, so we had a pretty heavy team to get the whole thing assembled. And we did it in time for the opening, even though Hervé was walking around getting worried!" Just to make his life easier, Newson decided to build a three-quarter sphere, so it was necessary to support the half-sphere while putting the lowest elements in place. The individual elements could be used as chairs, and the whole structure provided a frame for a series of theatrical and musical events. When he showed the same piece in Milan a couple of years later, this time as Bucky II, in a hard plastic version, he only built a hemisphere. But the piece is not just an exhibition item: in its hard version it was intended as an outdoor, weather-proof play structure.

—   Bucky perhaps represents both the summit and the limitations of Newson's achievement in Paris. While there he had met Benjamin de Haan and laid the plans for a future development, had started his work with Ikepod, both moves that were to take him from the particular, small project for design connoisseurs into a wider, truly industrial market, but Paris was too narrow a base. "The bureaucracy was difficult in France," he said once, "not that I was running a huge office or anything, but not having a French or even a European passport was a bore. I was glad to leave Paris, though now I quite miss the place and go back quite often!" And four years after the agency left Paris, Marc Newson Limited is planning to open a second office there.

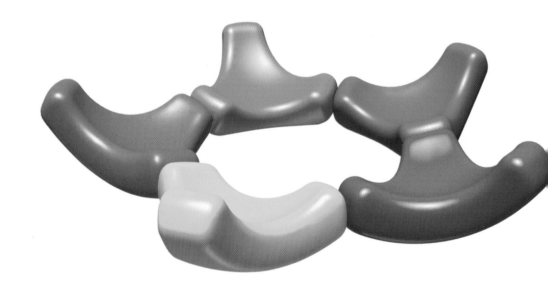

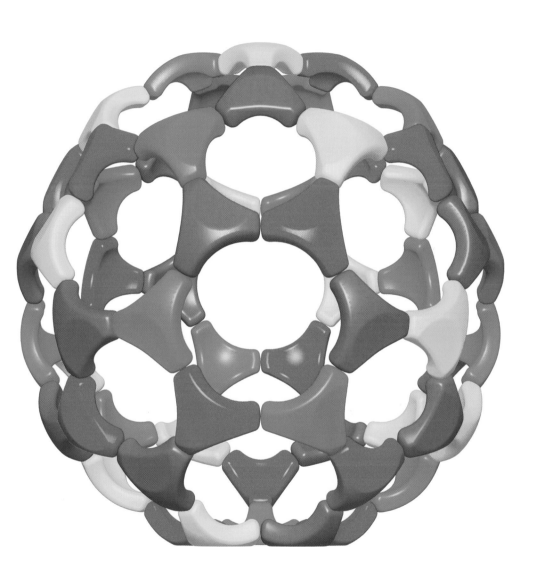

Marc Newson
—   In Control

—   Australia and Japan
—   Italy
—   France
—   For the Future

201   W&LT units,
      1996/7

202/3 WLT units and
       WLT chairs, 1996/7

For the Future

—   In a sense the Italian approac
to design is still, despite the use of sophisticated materials and
equipment, a craft one rather than an industrial one. It's about
conceiving an object that can be reproduced, rather than creatir
a reproductible object. The product comes first, not the market.
This works in the designer's favor if the designer's concerns are
mainly with formal values. One might think a designer intent on
controlling the totality of his work would prefer a craft solution,
but that is not always the case, at least for Newson. Take, for
example, the work he did for W&LT.

—   "Walter van Bierendoncke,"
Newson explains, "was one of a group of five fashion designers
who all came out of the same year from the Antwerp Academy ir
Belgium. When he came to see me in Paris, he was being backe
by Mustang, a very big German jeans company. He asked me
about designing the fittings for a range of shops they wanted to
open, some in independent sites, some in department stores,
and so on. It was very open-ended, and he wanted me to have as
much creative freedom as possible." Newson designed a modul
system of rail-mounted hanger units, in brightly-colored plastic,
together with a chair and a table. The point was to treat interior
design as industrial design. "I didn't have to deal with builders an
constructors," he says, "the whole shop arrived on the back of a
truck, you put down the rails, placed the modules and it was don
Depending on the size of the space you could have one, two or
four units or whatever. And they would go any way: on a fair stand
or even outdoors. You could fit out a shop, very cheaply, in under
a day." But you couldn't have one and a half modules, or place
them at odd angles, so Newson remained in control of the result
of his work, wherever it might be. "The units were like giant bread
bins, I used to think. They were very tough, made out of rotational
molded polypropylene by the largest garbage can manufacturer
Europe, kind of appropriate since W&LT stands for Wild and Leth
Trash!" About forty shops, and one trade fair stand, were fitted
using his designs. "It wasn't my first commission on an industrial
scale—the perfume bottle for Shiseido was an industrial design, ir
that sense. But it did involve using industrial processes to resolve
an interior design." By finding an unconventional and original
solution, Newson avoided the loss of integrity that a craft approac
risked.

—   However, even in that haven o
craft, Italy, times are changing. As Newson said in an interview wit
'Intramuros' journalist Pierre Doze, Italy is perhaps losing its
leading position, and the Milan Fair is no longer the center of the
furniture world. Others feel the same: Ross Lovegrove recently
told me that his selection for the International Design Yearbook
contained a lot less from Milan than used to be the case. "It's the
fault of the grand old men," Newson points out with a laugh, "like
Sottsass and Bellini who were eager to get the postwar industry
going and to set out their political and social agendas. They were

happy to work for low royalties and no payment in advance. Now we all respect their work, but these contractual conditions have in the meantime become a fixed precedent, and it's no longer appropriate. After all, the conception of the design is ninety percent of the work, and it comes first: to reward that only once manufacturing has started is the wrong way round."

— The point that Newson is making is that the paradigm of design has changed. The old model had the designer creating an object for the manufacturer, who made it and sold it as an individual, independent product. The public bought it because they liked the product, or admired the designer, or trusted the company, or whatever. Today the process is no longer so simple or so linear. Today manufacturers and designers (and an increasingly aware and sophisticated public) see the creation and sale of a product as an exchange of cultural values, not just monetary units. This has perhaps always been the case, that there has been an aesthetic and social nexus operating alongside the economic one. If so, it is a situation that today is much more visible, and more sharply focused. Commissioning and selling a new design is now seen as a process of mutual endorsement, in which the end result is a statement about the aspirations or values of all the parties involved. Put another way, the designer is no longer a tactician creating one product or even a series of products for a client, but part of the strategic team guiding a company forward in its dealings with the market, the public at large, and even itself, as we have seen in the case of the 021C for Ford. When Benjamin de Haan talks about "design as the third leg of business" it is to this strategic role for the designer that he refers.

— The place where this new realization about the potential of design is growing fastest is, according to Newson, the United States. "Some American companies may not have the same innate understanding of design that many European ones have," he explains, "but they are eager to learn, and so see the designer as a partner who should be rewarded for the conceptual content they bring in. Though it can sometimes be quite scary, to find myself sitting across a table from some guy who runs a multimillion dollar company and is expecting to learn something from me!" But Newson believes that once America gets its head around the concept of design, the rewards for designers—in terms of opportunity, not just money—will be very exciting. "It's the next place to be in terms of work opportunities," Newson says.

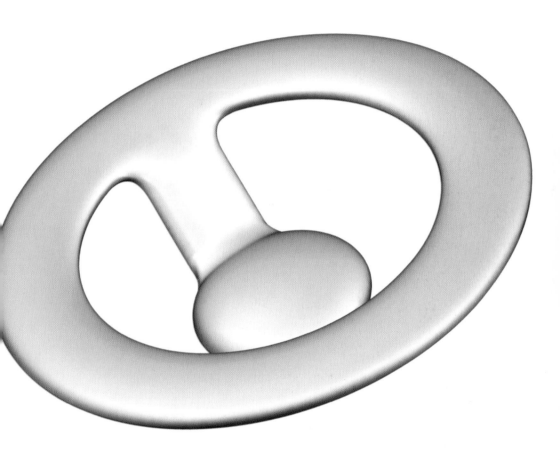

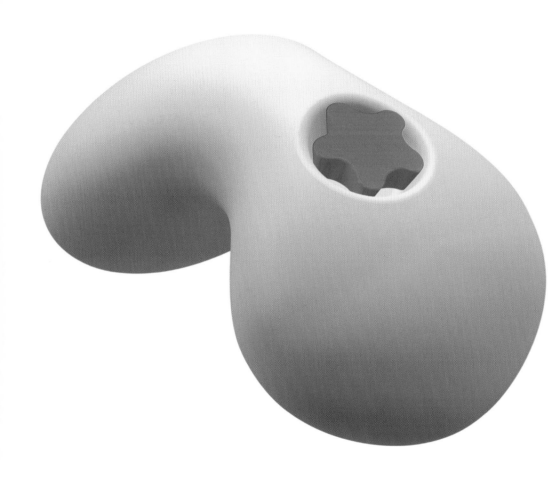

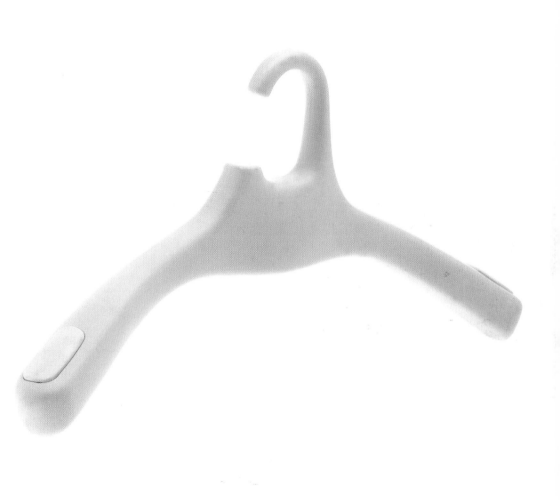

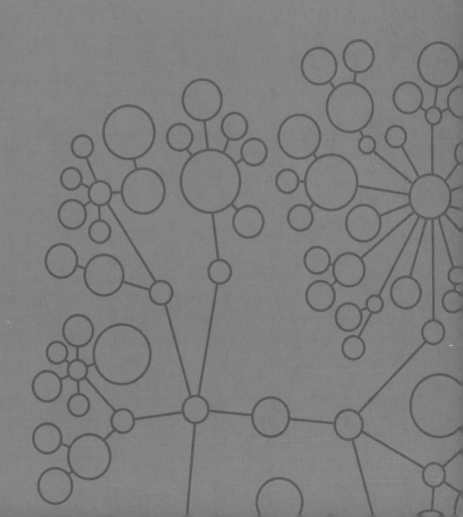

arc Newson
Travelling On

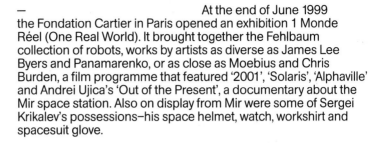

Russian spacesuit
acquired by Marc
Newson for the
Design Museum,
London

Marc Newson in a
Mig 29 fighter jet

— At the end of June 1999 the Fondation Cartier in Paris opened an exhibition 1 Monde Réel (One Real World). It brought together the Fehlbaum collection of robots, works by artists as diverse as James Lee Byers and Panamarenko, or as close as Moebius and Chris Burden, a film programme that featured '2001', 'Solaris', 'Alphaville' and Andrei Ujica's 'Out of the Present', a documentary about the Mir space station. Also on display from Mir were some of Sergei Krikalev's possessions—his space helmet, watch, workshirt and spacesuit glove.

— Sergei Krikalev is the man who has lived for the longest consecutive time in space: six months on the Mir station, among a number of other space missions. His experience was central to the main theme of the exhibition, which took its cue from a discussion between Albert Einstein and Rabindranath Tagore on whether the world—and the universe—exists independently of human perception, and whether if reality exists truth and beauty also exist independently. For Einstein, reality exists independently of humankind, and truths concerning that reality also exist, while for Tagore the world cannot exist apart from humanity's consciousness of it. The exhibition becomes an artistic and intellectual exploration of these ideas, in which science fiction and scientific fact also play a role.

— Marc Newson had created his Bucky sculpture at the Fondation Cartier in 1997, and he came to the opening of the 1 Monde Réel exhibition "because my friend, Fabrice Domercq, was also in the show." Here he also met Krikalev. Later Newson went to Star City, outside Moscow, where he had the chance to explore the mock-up of Mir that had been used as a training facility: he also got to take a flight in a Mig 29 fighter at the Gromov Flight Research Institute. On another of the many trips he has made to Baikonur and Star City, he watched Krikalev, now a mission controller, in charge of launching the rocket carrying the first human crew to the International Space Station. But meeting Krikalev did not just mean the excitement of meeting a real spaceman. It also meant understanding the realities of space.

— "When we were all having dinner with Krikalev after the exhibition," Newson says, "he mentioned this notebook that he used to hang around his neck, and which listed all the things he had to do each day to keep the station running. And his watch was in the exhibition: the strap had been mended by hand, lots of times." Talking of his time on Mir, Krikalev makes the point that the work schedule filled each day and often spilled into their free time on Sunday: "Sundays in space," he told Ujica, "are like Sundays on Earth, you have to fix the car or tidy the house. The only difference is you can't go out! And if you do leave the station, every gesture and movement is critical: errors are fatal. Each time I climbed out of the hatch I would turn to look at the Earth." Photos from Mir in the exhibition

showed instruments held in place with duct tape, and the clutter o
cables and hoses, harshly different from the polished interiors of
'2001', though reminiscent of the onboard chaos in 'Dark Star'. It i
in this sense of making do with what one has to hand that Newso
compares his early experience in Australia with conditions in
Russia. And seeing that Russian space science works–after all, M
stayed in orbit well beyond its planned lifespan–validates
Newson's continuing interest in space, as a metaphor, or a mode
Through meeting Krikalev space became a reality, in a sense, eve
though Mir's crew had a video of 'Solaris' on board, which Krikale
saw during the flight. And the Mir cosmonauts were trained to us
the on-board video cameras, from which footage Ujica's film was
made, by Vadim Yusov, the lighting cameraman on Tarkovsky's
film.

—   This understanding also
validates his working method: Newson, in a way like Krikalev,
starts any project in his notebook, with sketches and what J Mays
calls "scribbles." "I always start a design on paper. You can sketch
a curve on paper and know that it's just right, but you can't do tha
by a program in a computer: the curve isn't a function or a spline,
it's a freehand shape. But you can scan it into the computer
and develop it from there. You also have to understand how
your design is going to fit the manufacturing technology, or you
don't get the respect from the engineers you are working with.
Someone like Philippe Starck understands this: he wouldn't have
lasted so long if he were just a clever stylist. And having worked
myself in the automobile industry and seen how they approach
design, it doesn't surprise me that so many cars today look so
similar! And when I visit design schools or work with students I
feel there is too much reliance on the computer and not enough
understanding of technology, of how things are made." And the
attention to every detail necessary to stay alive and work in space
finds an echo in Newson's endless concern with detail in his
own work.

—   When Krikalev came back to
Earth he found the world around him had changed dramatically:
the former Soviet Union that had sent him into space had
disappeared in his absence. He found also that his memory of
the flights he had made faded with time: "They become more
and more unreal," he told Ujica, " more like fiction. Even now I
find it hard to realize that it is I that lived through that time." For
Newson as well the passage of time has brought change. The
new structure of his office means he designs rather than makes,
and his list of clients has moved from small, design-led companie
to major international groups such as Ford and Procter & Gamble
But what has been maintained, even honed by the experiences
he has gone through, has been an intense and individual eye for
form, and an aptitude to study and use technology creatively.

219   Marc Newson in
the Mir training
module at Star
City, 1999

220

Marc Newson
— Acknowledgments

221   Marc Newson
        Design Ltd,
        London 2001

Acknowledgments

This book is for Lucy, another young Australian, with love.

Chris Barrett at 'Graphics International' magazine in London first encouraged me to meet Marc Newson, and the idea of this book grew from that meeting, though I have admired Marc's work for the last decade. Talking with creative people about their work is interesting, and when the people are committed, intelligent and witty as well, as Marc is, it is fascinating. I'm very grateful to Marc and his colleagues at Marc Newson Design Ltd., for their time and their enthusiasm for this book.

Mark Farrow and Jonathon Jeffrey at Farrow Design, who created the graphic language for the book, showed equal enthusiasm and it was a real pleasure to work with them.

Other friends, clients and colleagues of Marc, including in particular J Mays, Ross Lovegrove and Oliver Ike, took time to talk to me about him, and I am very grateful to them.

To Charles Miers and his colleagues at Universe, thanks for their patience and support.

Conway Lloyd Morgan
London, December 2001

The author and the publishers would like to thank the following photographers, artists, designers and agencies whose work appears in this book:

Richard Allan, Karin Catt, Imagination, Sameli Rantanen, John Ross, Sue Stafford, Solid State, Toast and Tom Vack

We also thank the following companies for whom Marc has designed:

Alessi, Cappelini, Flos, Ford Motor Company, Idée, Ikepod, Magis Moroso, Newlines and Vidal Sassoon

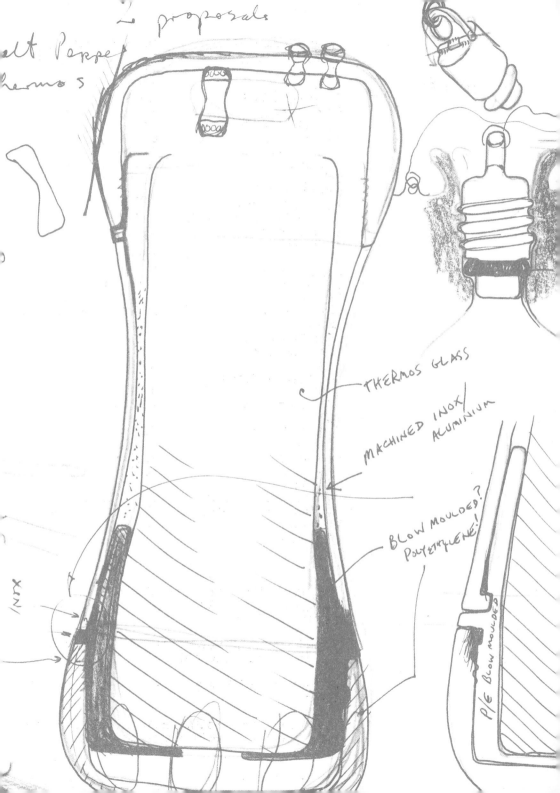

Salt Pepper ~ proposals

~ hermos

THERMOS GLASS

MACHINED INOX/
ALUMINIUM

BLOW MOULDED?
POLYETHYLENE!

INOX

P/E BLOW MOULDED

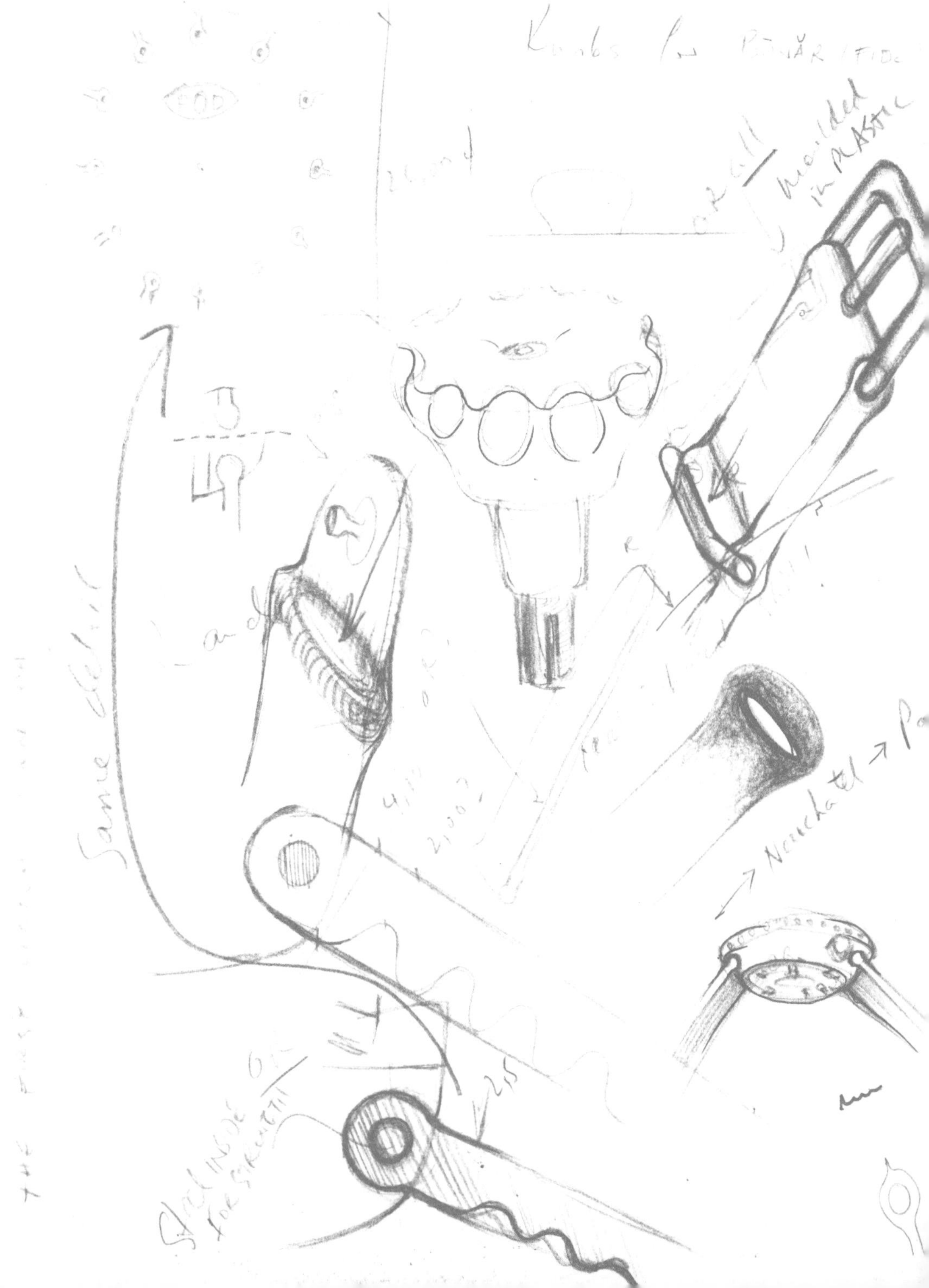
moulded in PLASTIC
Same detail
Neuchatel →

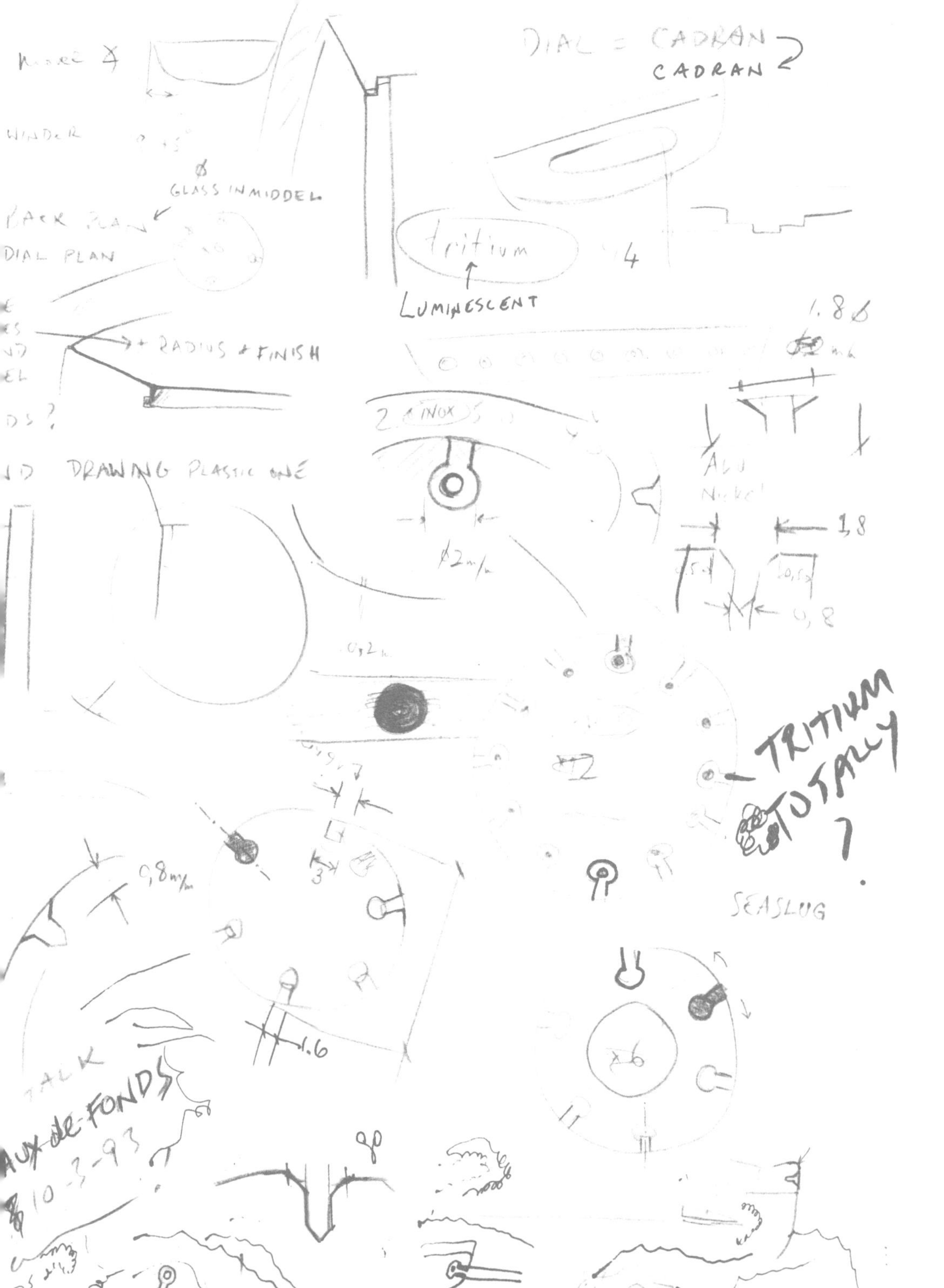

MODEL 7

WINDER

GLASS IN MIDDEL

DIAL = CADRAN
CADRAN 2

BACK PLATE
DIAL PLAN

tritium

4

LUMINESCENT

1.86

RADIUS & FINISH

DS ?

2 X INOX 5

ALU
Nickel

1,8

0,8

JD DRAWING PLASTIC ONE

Ø 2m/m

0,2h

Ø 2

TRITIUM
TOTALLY
?

SEASLUG

0,8 m/m

X 6

1,6

TALK

AUX de FONDS

10-3-93

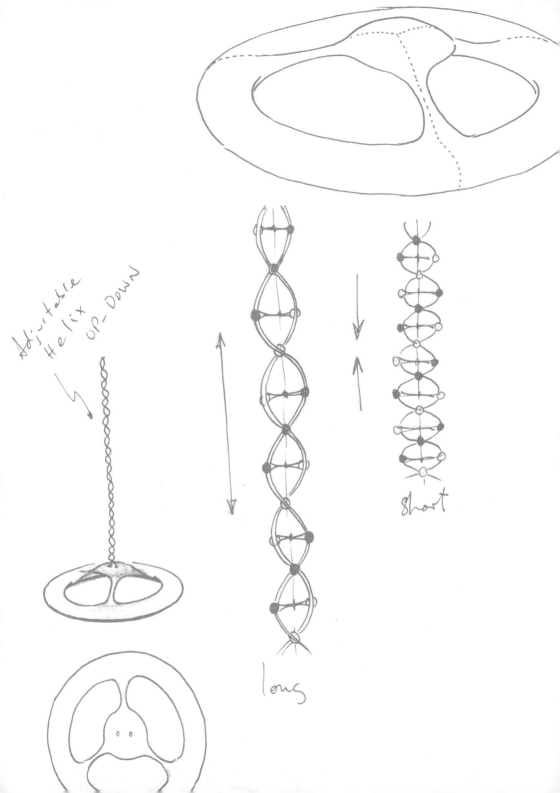

Adjustable
Helix
UP–Down

Long

Short

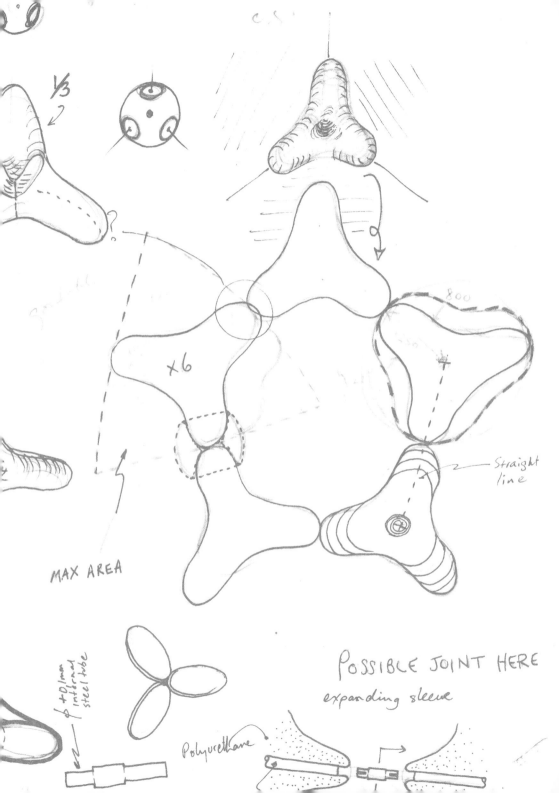

1/3

800

×6

MAX AREA

Straight
line

POSSIBLE JOINT HERE
expanding sleeve

ϕ +0.1mm
internal
steel tube

Polyurethane

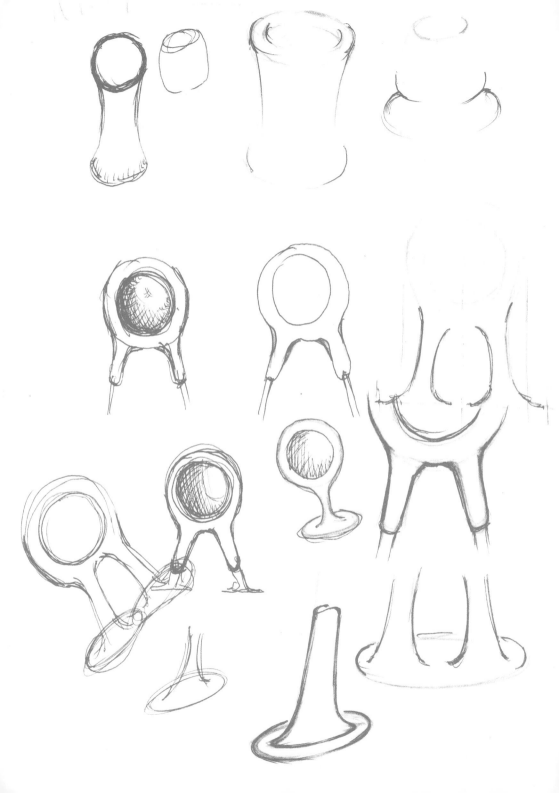

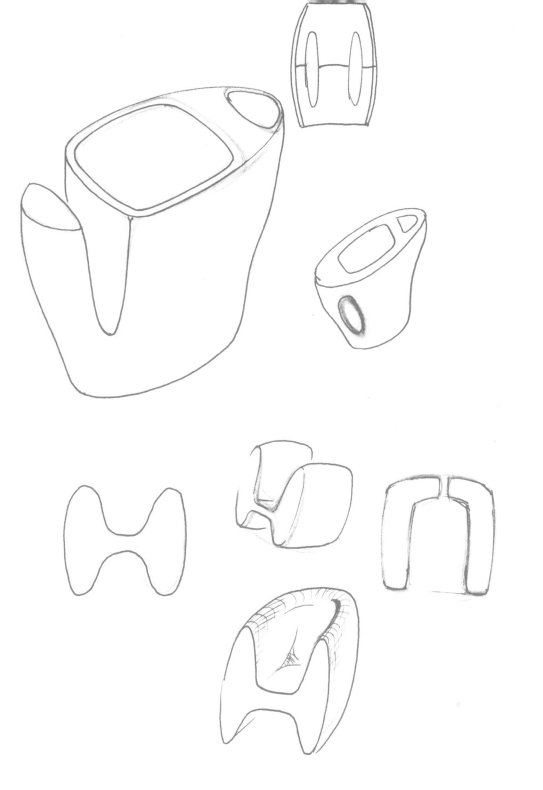

bottle opener

oil + vinegar
+ salt + pepper

my shape

stainless steel

or silicone
transparent
URETHANE ...

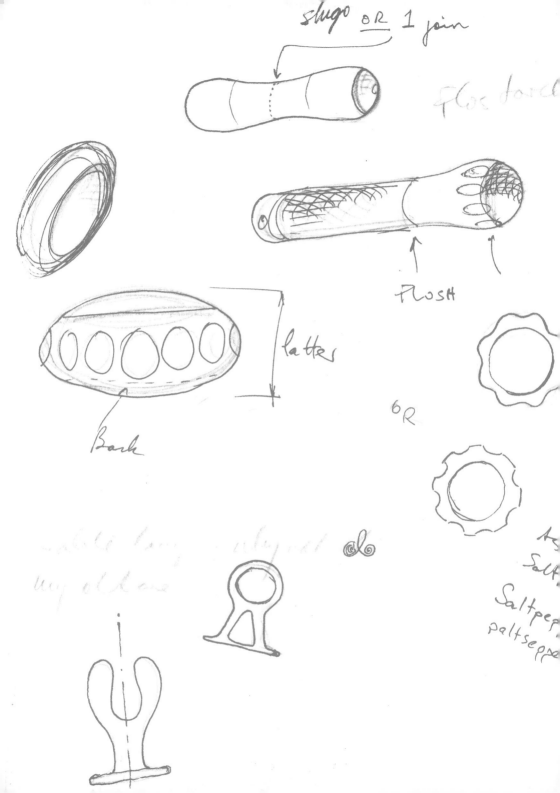

slugo OR 1 join

Floc dord

PLUSH

latter

Bork

OR

Saltpep
paltseppe

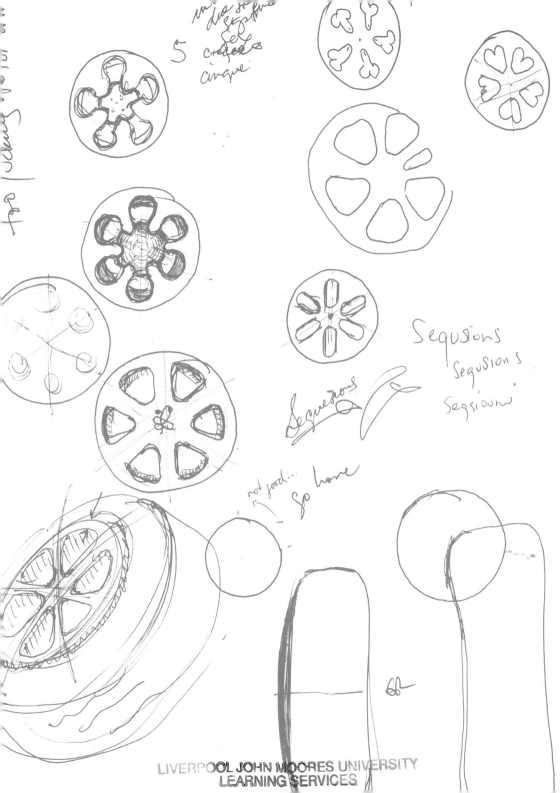

5

Sequsions

Sequsions

Sequsions

Sequsions

Sequsions

not good... go home

1.

2.

3.

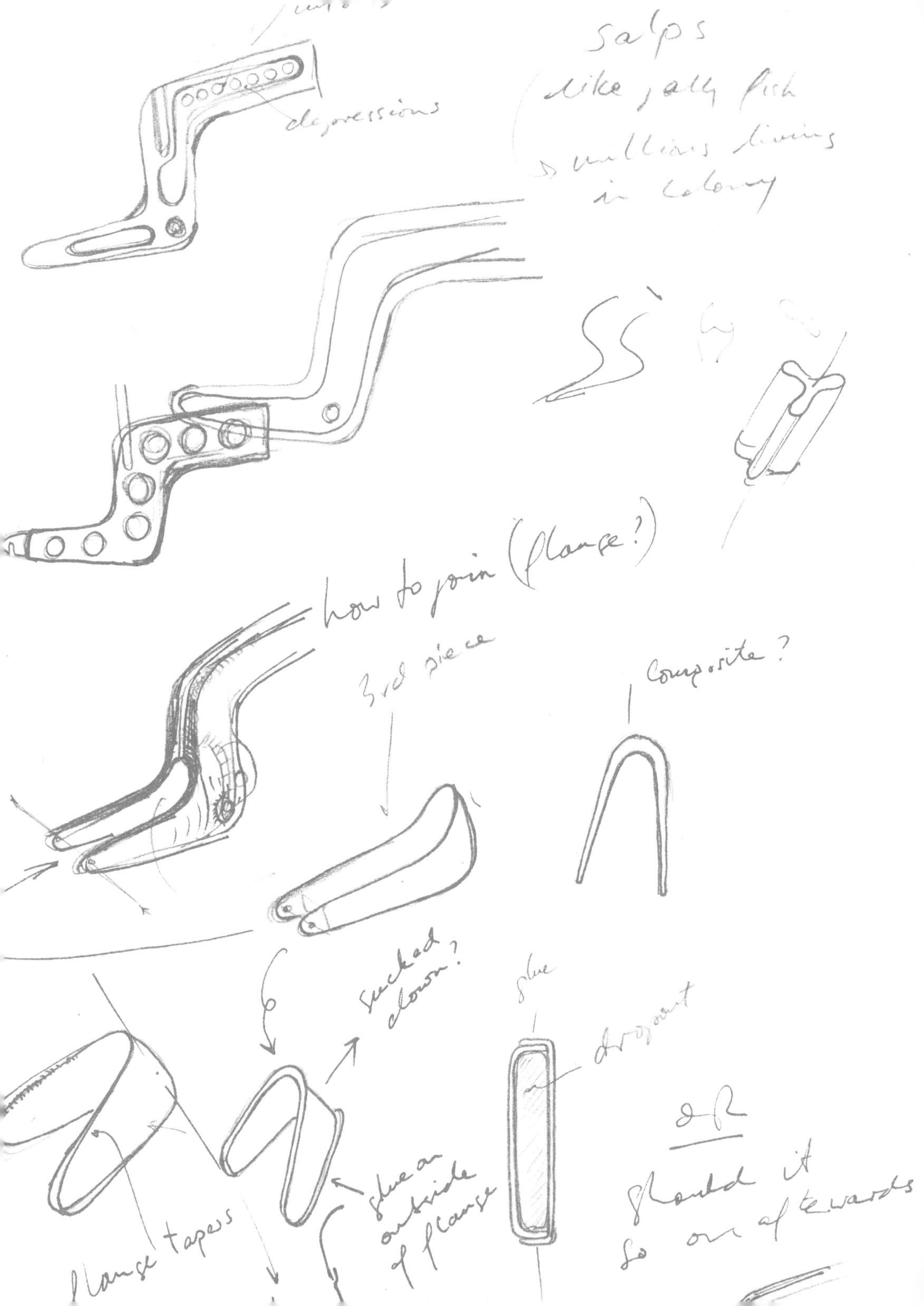

depressions

salps
like jelly fish
→ multiins living
in colony

how to join (flange?)

3rd piece

composite?

glue

dropout

sucked down?

glue on
outside
of flange

should it
be on afterwards

flange tapes

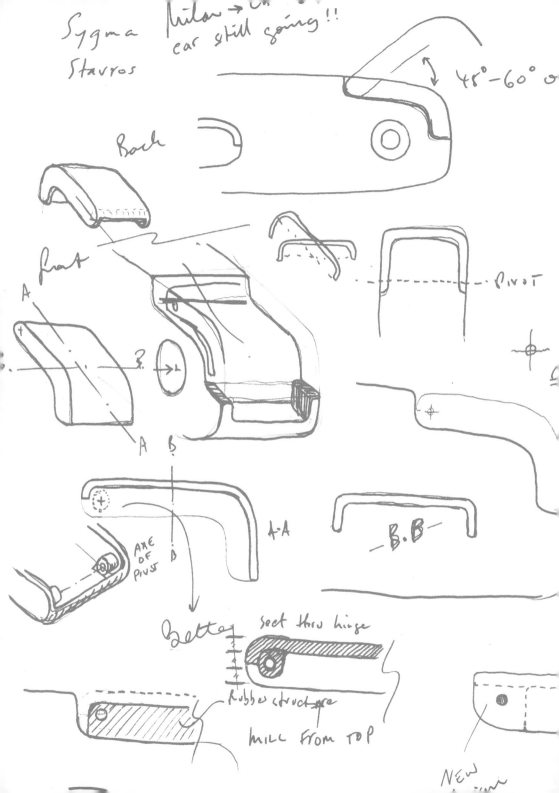

Sygma
Stavros

Milan → ...
ear still going !!

45°–60°

Back

front

A
A
2.
1
A
B

AXE
OF
PIVOT

A·A

B·B

Pivot

Better

seet thru hinge

Rubber structure

MILL FROM TOP

NEW

9306000

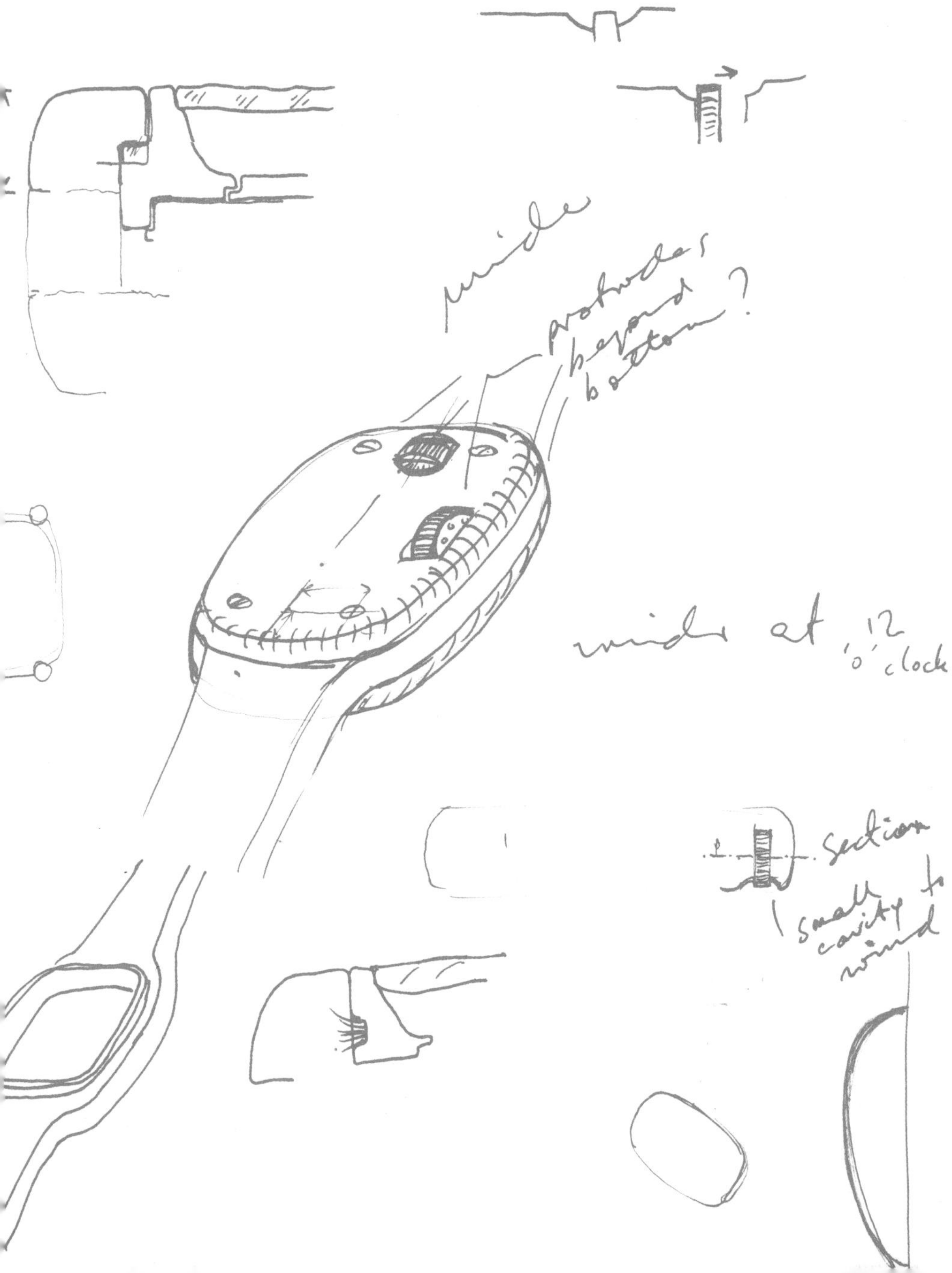

guide

protrudes
beyond
bottom ?

guide at 12
'o' clock

Section

small cavity to
wind